Betty Crocker's
Baking Classics

Random House, Inc. New York

Dear Friend,

Gold Medal® flour has played an important role in the cooking heritage of America. With this cookbook, we salute the centennial of Gold Medal by presenting the best Gold Medal recipes of 100 years.

We have included recipes which were popular advertising features of the early 1900s, during the Depression and in the 1950s. Some are down-home recipes like your grandmother made...just plain good eating. Others are glorious creations, perfect for special occasions and holidays. We also have taken great recipes from some of our firm's old cookbooks, published as early as 1880.

As you use this cookbook, you will notice that some of the recipes bear a Gold Medal insignia. These are among our oldest recipes, dating from 1880 to the 1920s when the company established its first test kitchen, ancestor of today's modern Betty Crocker Kitchens.

Many recipes, especially the very old ones, had to be rewritten in the contemporary Betty Crocker style. We adapted them for today's ingredients and cooking equipment; we established precise cooking times and temperatures; and we retested every recipe to assure you top quality results.

A photograph of each prepared recipe is included here so that you know exactly what to expect. In addition, many step-by-step photographs will guide you through selected recipe preparation.

In its 100 years, Gold Medal has made history numerous times. Throughout the book are historical highlights about especially notable recipes and about Gold Medal milestones.

All the recipes in this book have been developed and tested exclusively with Gold Medal flour. We invite you to read the book, try the recipes and enjoy the assurance of baking success with Gold Medal "Kitchen-tested"® flour.

Cordially,

Betty Crocker

Originally published in 1979 by General Mills, Inc. as the Gold Medal Century of Success Cookbook and distributed in response to Gold Medal® flour offers. Now available in bookstores for the first time.

® Reg. T.M. of General Mills, Inc.

Library of Congress Cataloging in Publication Data   Crocker, Betty, pseud. Betty Crocker's Baking Classics.

Includes index.   1. Baking.   I. Title.   II. Title: Baking Classics.   TX763.C75   641.8'65   80-6043   ISBN 0-394-51883-7

Manufactured in the United States of America   24689753   First Trade Edition

Contents

The Medal of Gold

Winning the Gold Medal at the Millers' International Exhibition in 1880 was a great victory for Cadwallader C. Washburn of Minneapolis. At that time, Washburn had been in the milling business for just 14 years. His first mill, called "Washburn's Folly" by some, was a huge six-story stone structure with 12 pairs of millstones.

People said it was not possible for the region to use all the flour produced by such a large mill. Washburn, however, ignored public sentiment, because he viewed the entire nation — even the world — as his market. To accomplish his ambitious goals, Washburn encouraged innovation, installing the most modern equipment available and seeking out experts in management and milling.

In 1879 Washburn had built the first complete automatic roller mill. That same year he joined with John Crosby, Charles Martin and William H. Dunwoody to form Washburn, Crosby and Company to operate the Washburn mills.

In 1880 Washburn Crosby participated in the first Millers' International Exhibition, held in Cincinnati, Ohio. Attended by millers from around the world, the exhibition offered awards for the best flour. Washburn Crosby took the three top prizes: the Bronze Medal for "Parisian" Flour, the Silver Medal for "Extra" Flour and the Gold Medal for "Superlative" Flour.

After winning the esteemed Gold Medal award at the Millers' International Exhibition in 1880, Washburn Crosby began selling "Gold Medal" Flour.

The Best Gold Medal Recipes of 100 Years

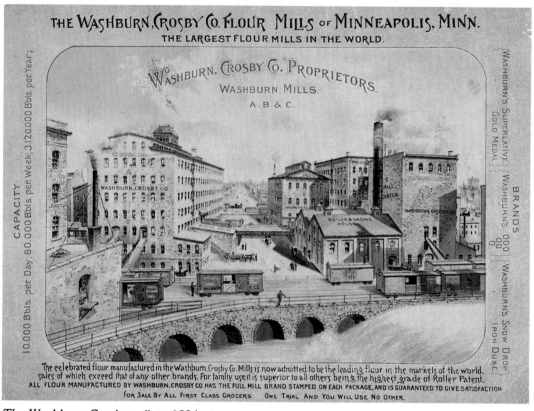

The Washburn Crosby mills in 1894

The history of Gold Medal flour is a story of innovation and pioneering spirit.

Washburn Crosby Company, millers of Gold Medal flour, encouraged milling inventions which improved the quality and appearance of flour. In 1893 they established the first flour testing room for checking flour quality and uniformity. By 1910 the testing room became a complete bakery where daily baking tests were conducted. And in 1921 the company hired its first home economist as well to provide testing of the flour.

Shortly after the turn of the century, Washburn Crosby, along with other millers, began seeking more sanitary packaging for flour. They switched from fabric bags to cartons, wrapped shells and fiber cans. The scarcity of fabric because of World War I further emphasized the need for new packaging, and millers turned to paper bags.

Also during the early 1900s, Washburn Crosby began looking for ways to ensure more efficient delivery of Gold Medal flour to consumers everywhere. Other mills were established and, beginning in 1928, James Ford Bell brought together a number of flour mills to form one company. The largest of these was Washburn Crosby, and the oldest was West Coast's Sperry Flour Company, founded in 1852. These companies formed the world's largest flour miller ... General Mills, Inc.

Washburn Crosby's 1922 test kitchen

Service to Consumers

Washburn Crosby's one-person test kitchen of the early 1920s has evolved to the Betty Crocker Food & Nutrition Center which consolidates the Betty Crocker Kitchens, Nutrition, and Publications & Publicity in one department. It provides complete, coordinated information services to food editors, health professionals, home economists and supermarket consumer advisors.

Gold Medal recipe service over the years has responded to consumer needs of the time. During the depression years, recipes were developed to fit drastically reduced food budgets. And when World War II created food shortages, Gold Medal recipes helped consumers make the most of available foods.

With the enrichment of flour in the early 1940s came a growing interest in nutrition. General Mills provided nutrition information in advertisements, with booklets and on the radio. Special programs were established for elementary school children, home economics students and 4-H club members.

Over the years, a number of "firsts" in service have been associated with Gold Medal ... radio's first consumer food service program, the one-bowl cake-making method, a new way to make pastry using liquid shortening, chiffon cake and pre-sifted flour, just to name a few.

Cookbooks Since 1880

In the same year that the Gold Medal brand was introduced, Washburn Crosby also introduced its first cookbook ... Miss Parloa's New Cook Book of 1880. Next came the Washburn Crosby Co.'s New Cook Book of 1894. That was followed by the Gold Medal Cook Book of the early 1900s. Since that time, there has been a continuing flow of cookbooks to aid consumers in their daily meal preparation.

Recipes in the company's early cookbooks — as in other cookbooks of the time— often provided vague directions and ingredient quantities.

Washburn Crosby's newly organized home service department in the 1920s changed all this with standardized, fully tested recipes and directions. Cookbooks that followed provided greater service to consumers and greater assurance of success.

The efforts of those first home economists laid the foundation for the recipe development procedures used with today's Gold Medal recipes. All are created according to well-defined standards for quality and good taste. They are tested thoroughly and written in a style which is easy to use and familiar to Gold Medal users everywhere.

One of today's Betty Crocker test kitchens

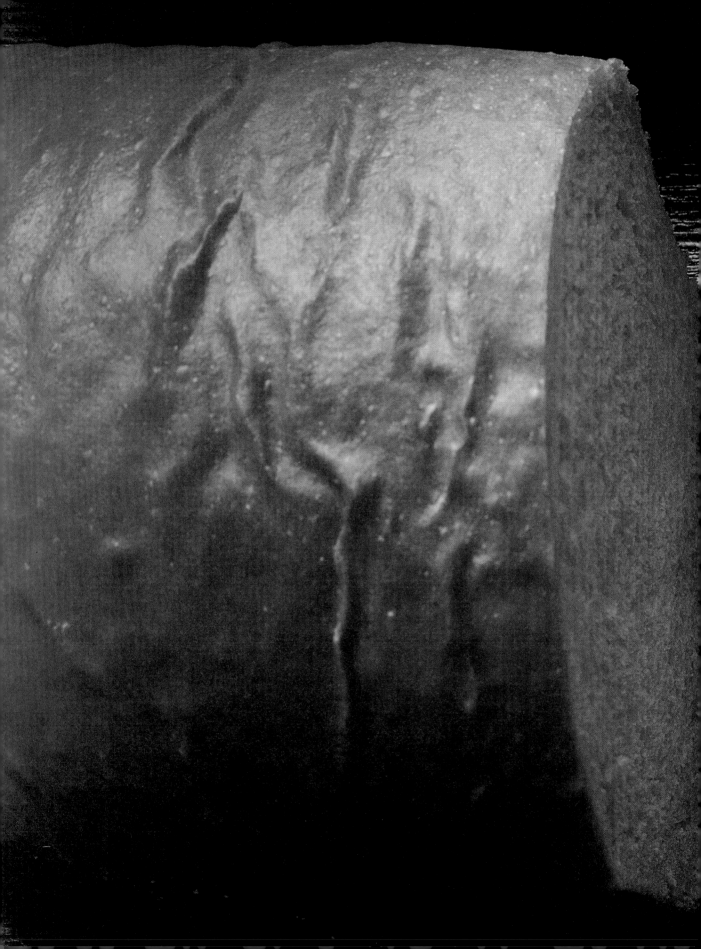

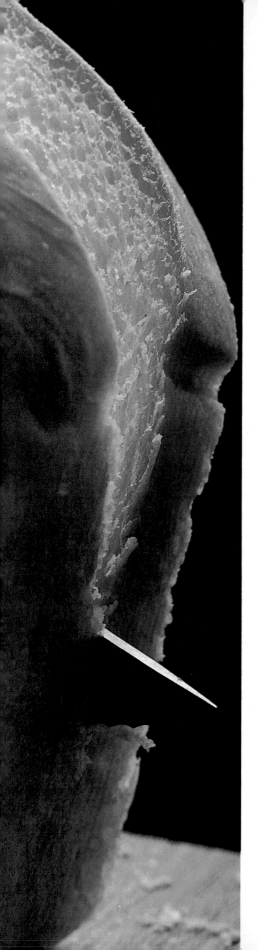

COUNTRY CRUST BREAD

2 packages active dry yeast
2 cups warm water
(105 to 115°)
½ cup sugar
1 tablespoon salt
2 eggs

¼ cup vegetable oil
6 to 6½ cups Gold Medal
all-purpose flour*
Vegetable oil
Margarine or butter,
softened

Dissolve yeast in warm water in large mixing bowl. Stir in sugar, salt, eggs, ¼ cup oil and 3 cups of the flour. Beat until smooth. Mix in enough remaining flour to make dough easy to handle.

Turn dough onto lightly floured surface; knead until smooth and elastic, 8 to 10 minutes. Place in greased bowl; turn greased side up. (At this point, dough can be refrigerated 3 to 4 days.) Cover; let rise in warm place until double, about 1 hour. (Dough is ready if indentation remains when touched.)

Punch down dough; divide into halves. Roll each half into rectangle, 18×9 inches. Roll up tightly, beginning at 9-inch side. Press with thumbs to seal after each turn. Pinch edge firmly to seal. Press each end with side of hand to seal; fold ends under loaf. Place loaf, seam side down, in greased baking pan, 9×5×3 inches. Brush with oil. Let rise until double, about 1 hour.

Heat oven to 375°. Bake until loaves are deep golden brown and sound hollow when tapped, 30 to 35 minutes. Remove from pans. Brush with margarine; cool on wire rack.   2 loaves.

*If using self-rising flour, omit salt.

Cinnamon-Raisin Bread: Divide dough into halves. Knead ½ cup raisins into each half. Roll each half into rectangle, 18×9 inches. Brush with oil. Mix ½ cup sugar and 1 tablespoon ground cinnamon; sprinkle over rectangles. Continue as directed.

Fill large bowl ⅔ full with hot water; cover with wire rack. Place bowl of dough on rack. Cover completely. Replace cooled water with hot after 30 minutes.

Punch down center of dough once firmly with fist. Pull edges of dough to center and remove from bowl; divide into halves.

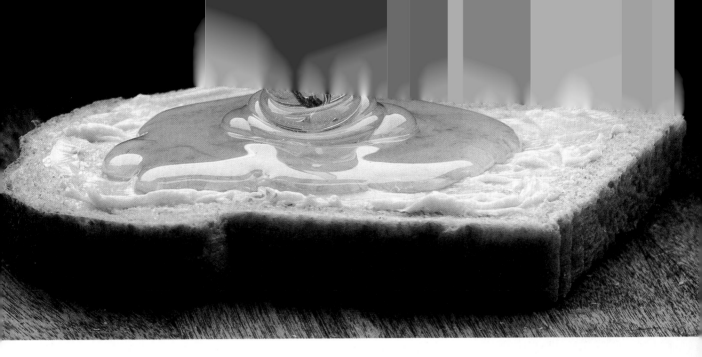

HONEY-WHOLE WHEAT BREAD

2	packages active dry yeast	3	cups Gold Medal whole wheat flour
½	cup warm water (105 to 115°)	3	to 4 cups Gold Medal all-purpose flour*
⅓	cup honey		Margarine or butter, softened
¼	cup shortening		
1	tablespoon salt		
1¾	cups warm water		

Dissolve yeast in ½ cup warm water in large mixing bowl. Stir in honey, shortening, salt, 1¾ cups warm water and the whole wheat flour. Beat until smooth. Mix in enough all-purpose flour to make dough easy to handle.

Turn dough onto lightly floured surface; knead until smooth and elastic, about 10 minutes. Place in greased bowl; turn greased side up. Cover; let rise in warm place until double, about 1 hour. (Dough is ready if indentation remains when touched.)

Punch down dough; divide into halves. Flatten each half with hands or rolling pin into rectangle, 18×9 inches. Fold crosswise into thirds, overlapping the 2 sides. Roll up tightly, beginning at one of the open ends. Press with thumbs to seal after each turn. Pinch edge firmly to seal. Press each end with side of hand to seal; fold ends under loaf. Place loaves, seam sides down, in 2 greased baking pans, 9×5×3 or 8½×4½×2½ inches. Brush with margarine; sprinkle with whole wheat flour or crushed oats if desired. Let rise until double, about 1 hour.

Heat oven to 375°. Bake until loaves are deep golden brown and sound hollow when tapped, 40 to 45 minutes. Remove from pans; cool on wire rack.   2 loaves.

*If using self-rising flour, decrease salt to 1 teaspoon.

Washburn Crosby's first long-run advertising campaign was built around the slogan "Eventually — Why Not Now?" First used in 1907, the slogan appeared on billboards, on flour bags and in the company's magazine and newspaper advertisements as late as the early 1950s. The slogan attracted much public attention, and since has been associated with Gold Medal flour.

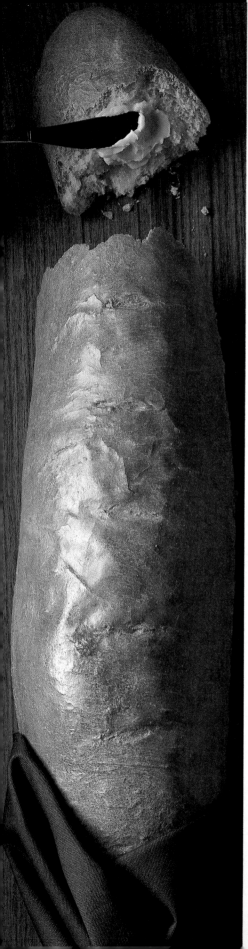

FRENCH BREAD

1 package active dry yeast	3½ to 4 cups Gold Medal all-purpose flour
1¼ cups warm water (105 to 115°)	1 tablespoon cornmeal Cold water
1½ teaspoons salt	1 egg white
1 tablespoon shortening	2 tablespoons cold water

Dissolve yeast in warm water in large mixing bowl. Stir in salt, shortening and 1½ cups of the flour. Beat with spoon until smooth. Mix in enough remaining flour (first with spoon, then by hand) to make dough easy to handle.

Turn dough onto lightly floured surface; knead until smooth and elastic, about 5 minutes. Place in greased bowl; turn greased side up. Cover; let rise in warm place until double, 1½ to 2 hours. (Dough is ready if indentation remains when touched.)

Punch down dough; round up and let rise until almost double, about 45 minutes. Punch down; cover and let rest 15 minutes. Sprinkle with cornmeal. Roll dough into rectangle, 15×10 inches. Roll up tightly, beginning at 15-inch side. Pinch edge firmly to seal. Roll gently back and forth to taper ends. Place loaf on lightly greased cookie sheet. If desired, make ¼-inch slashes across loaf at 2-inch intervals. Brush with cold water. Let rise about 1½ hours. Brush with cold water.

Heat oven to 375°. Bake 20 minutes. Beat egg white and 2 tablespoons cold water slightly; brush over loaf. Bake 25 minutes longer. Remove from cookie sheet; cool on wire rack.

ITALIAN BREADSTICKS

1 package active dry yeast	2 to 2¼ cups Gold Medal all-purpose flour
⅔ cup warm water (105 to 115°)	Vegetable or olive oil
1 tablespoon sugar	1 egg white
1 teaspoon salt	1 tablespoon water
¼ cup vegetable or olive oil	Coarse salt or toasted sesame seed

Dissolve yeast in warm water in large mixing bowl. Stir in sugar, 1 teaspoon salt, ¼ cup oil and 1 cup of the flour. Beat until smooth. Mix in enough remaining flour to make dough easy to handle.

Turn dough onto lightly floured surface; knead until smooth and elastic, about 5 minutes. Shape dough into roll, 10 inches long. Cut into 36 equal parts. Roll each part into rope, 8 inches long for thick breadsticks, 10 inches long for thin breadsticks. Place about 1 inch apart on greased cookie sheet. Brush with oil. Cover; let rise in warm place about 20 minutes.

Heat oven to 350°. Beat egg white and 1 tablespoon water slightly; brush over breadsticks and sprinkle with coarse salt. Bake until golden brown, 20 to 25 minutes.   3 dozen breadsticks.

GRANOLA-YOGURT BREAD

2 packages active dry yeast
½ cup warm water
   (105 to 115°)
2 teaspoons sugar
1 cup warm water
1 carton (8 ounces) plain
   yogurt

1 tablespoon salt
5 to 5½ cups Gold Medal
   all-purpose flour
2 cups Nature Valley®
   granola (any flavor)
Margarine or butter,
   softened

Dissolve yeast in ½ cup warm water. Stir in sugar. Let stand until bubbly and double in volume, about 10 minutes. Mix 1 cup warm water, the yogurt and salt in large mixer bowl. Stir in yeast mixture. Beat in 3 cups of the flour on medium speed, scraping bowl occasionally, 2 minutes. Mix in granola and enough remaining flour to make dough easy to handle.

Turn dough onto lightly floured surface; knead until smooth and elastic, about 10 minutes. Place in greased bowl; turn greased side up. Cover; let rise in warm place until double, about 1 hour. (Dough is ready if indentation remains when touched.)

Punch down dough; divide into halves. Shape each half into oval; place on lightly greased cookie sheet. Brush with margarine. Let rise until double, about 40 minutes.

Heat oven to 375°. Bake until loaves are golden brown and sound hollow when tapped, 30 to 35 minutes. Remove from cookie sheet. Brush with margarine; cool on wire rack. 2 loaves.

SALLY LUNN

2 packages active dry yeast	1½ teaspoons salt
½ cup warm water (105 to 115°)	2 eggs
1½ cups lukewarm milk (scalded then cooled)	¼ cup shortening
2 tablespoons sugar	5½ cups Gold Medal all-purpose flour*

Dissolve yeast in warm water in large mixing bowl. Stir in remaining ingredients. Beat until smooth. Cover; let rise in warm place until double, about 1 hour.

Stir down batter by beating about 25 strokes. Spread in greased tube pan, 10×4 inches. Let rise to within 1 inch of top of pan, about 45 minutes.

Heat oven to 350°. Bake until loaf is golden brown and crusty, 45 to 50 minutes. Remove from pan; serve warm.   16 servings.

*If using self-rising flour, omit salt.

Sally Lunn appears in many Gold Medal cookbooks beginning with the _Gold Medal Flour Cook Book_ of the early 1900s. A popular tea bread in Colonial America, Sally Lunn was originally a bun made in a bake shop of Bath, England. Some say the bread was named for Sally Lunn, who worked in the shop.

Spread batter in greased tube pan, 10×4 inches.

Let batter rise over bowl of hot water, about 1 hour.

Lift bread from pan; loosen bottom with spatula.

OATMEAL-MOLASSES BREAD

¾ cup boiling water	1 egg
½ cup regular oats	2¾ cups Gold Medal
3 tablespoons shortening	all-purpose flour*
¼ cup light molasses	1 egg white, slightly beaten
2 teaspoons salt	¼ cup regular oats, crushed
1 package active dry yeast	¼ teaspoon salt
¼ cup warm water	
(105 to 115°)	

Washburn Crosby hired its first home economist in 1921. Within a year, the one-person kitchen was expanded to more spacious and better equipped quarters, staffed by three home economists. In those days, the company sponsored cooking schools in conjunction with women's clubs and newspapers. The home economists developed the "Kitchen-tested" recipes featured in Gold Medal advertisements. They also provided cooking advice to home economics teachers and 4-H club leaders.

Mix boiling water, ½ cup oats, the shortening, molasses and 2 teaspoons salt in large mixer bowl; cool to lukewarm. Dissolve yeast in warm water. Stir yeast, egg and 1½ cups of the flour into the oat mixture. Beat on medium speed, scraping bowl frequently, 2 minutes. Stir in remaining flour until smooth.

Smooth and pat batter in greased 2-pound coffee can with floured hands. Brush top with egg white. Mix ¼ cup oats and ¼ teaspoon salt; sprinkle over top. Let rise in warm place until double, about 1½ hours.

Heat oven to 375°. Bake until loaf is brown and sounds hollow when tapped, 50 to 55 minutes. (If loaf is browning too quickly, cover with foil during last 15 minutes of baking.) Remove from can; cool on wire rack.

*If using self-rising flour, omit salt.

16

SWISS CHEESE LOAF

1 package active dry yeast	½ cup vegetable oil
¼ cup warm water (105 to 115°)	3 eggs
¼ cup lukewarm milk (scalded then cooled)	2¾ cups Gold Medal all-purpose flour*
1½ teaspoons sugar	1 cup ¼-inch cubes Swiss cheese (about 8 ounces)
1 teaspoon salt	

Dissolve yeast in warm water in large mixer bowl. Stir in milk, sugar, salt, oil, eggs and 1½ cups of the flour. Beat on medium speed, scraping bowl occasionally, 10 minutes. Stir in remaining flour with spoon until smooth. Cover; let rise in warm place until double, about 1 hour.

Stir down batter by beating about 25 strokes; gently work in cheese until evenly distributed. Shape into ball; place in greased pie plate, 9 × 1¼ inches. Let rise until double, about 1 hour.

Heat oven to 375°. Bake until golden brown, about 30 minutes. Remove from plate; cool on wire rack.

*If using self-rising flour, omit salt.

American Cheese Loaf: Substitute American cheese for the Swiss cheese.

CHILI PEPPER-CHEESE BREAD

1 package active dry yeast	2½ cups Gold Medal all-purpose flour*
½ cup warm water (105 to 115°)	½ cup cornmeal
½ cup lukewarm milk (scalded then cooled)	1 cup shredded hot pepper cheese (about 4 ounces)
⅔ cup margarine or butter, softened	2 to 4 tablespoons chopped green chilies, drained on paper towels
2 eggs	Cornmeal
1 teaspoon salt	

Dissolve yeast in warm water in large mixing bowl. Stir in milk, margarine, eggs, salt and 1 cup of the flour. Beat on low speed, scraping bowl constantly, 30 seconds. Beat on medium speed, scraping bowl occasionally, 2 minutes. Stir in remaining flour, ½ cup cornmeal, the cheese and chilies. Scrape batter from side of bowl. Cover; let rise in warm place until double, about 30 minutes.

Stir down batter by beating about 25 strokes. Spread in greased 2-quart round casserole. Cover; let rise until double, about 40 minutes.

Heat oven to 375°. Sprinkle loaf with cornmeal. Bake until loaf is brown and sounds hollow when tapped, 40 to 45 minutes. Remove from casserole; cool on wire rack. To serve, cut into wedges with serrated knife.

*If using self-rising flour, omit salt.

Onion-Dill Bread: Omit cornmeal, cheese and chilies. Increase flour to 3 cups. Stir in ¼ cup chopped onion and 1 tablespoon dried dill weed with the second addition of flour. Brush top of loaf with margarine or butter, softened, and sprinkle with sesame seed or poppy seed before baking.

Left to right: Hamburger Buns, Crescent Rolls, Parker House Rolls, Braided Dinner Rolls

Miss Parloa's New Cook Book *of 1880, Washburn Crosby's first cookbook, included a recipe for Parker House Rolls which can be made from Potato Refrigerator Dough. Sometimes called pocketbook rolls, they originated at The Parker House, a Boston restaurant founded in 1855.*

POTATO REFRIGERATOR DOUGH

1	package active dry yeast	2	eggs
1½	cups warm water (105 to 115°)	1	cup lukewarm mashed potatoes*
⅔	cup sugar	7	to 7½ cups Gold Medal all-purpose flour**
1½	teaspoons salt		
⅔	cup shortening		

Dissolve yeast in warm water in large mixing bowl. Stir in sugar, salt, shortening, eggs, potatoes and 4 cups of the flour. Beat until smooth. Mix in enough remaining flour to make dough easy to handle.

Turn dough onto lightly floured surface; knead until smooth and elastic, about 5 minutes. Place in greased bowl; turn greased side up. Cover bowl tightly; refrigerate at least 8 hours but no longer than 5 days.

Punch down dough. Shape, let rise and bake as directed in the following recipes and for Apricot Cream Cake (page 25).

*Potato Buds® mashed potatoes can be substituted for the mashed potatoes; prepare as directed on package for 2 servings.

**If using self-rising flour, omit salt.

18

BRAIDED DINNER ROLLS

⅓ Potato Refrigerator Dough (opposite)
1 egg
1 tablespoon water
¾ teaspoon poppy seed
¾ teaspoon sesame seed

Divide dough into 18 equal parts. Roll each part into rope, 7 inches long, on lightly floured surface. Place groups of 3 ropes each close together on lightly greased cookie sheet. Braid ropes gently and loosely. Do not stretch. Pinch ends to fasten; tuck under securely. Let rise until double, 45 to 60 minutes.

Heat oven to 375°. Beat egg and water slightly; brush over braids. Sprinkle each of 3 braids with ¼ teaspoon poppy seed and each of remaining 3 braids with ¼ teaspoon sesame seed. Bake until golden brown, about 15 minutes. 6 rolls.

PARKER HOUSE ROLLS

Prepare Potato Refrigerator Dough (opposite). Divide into halves (refrigerate 1 half for future use or use for Crescent Rolls, below). Divide remaining half of dough into halves. Roll 1 half into rectangle, 13×9 inches. Cut into 3-inch circles; brush with margarine or butter, softened. Fold each so top half overlaps slightly. Press edges together. Place close together in greased round baking pan, 9×1½ inches. Brush with margarine or butter, softened. Repeat with remaining dough. Let rise until double, 45 to 60 minutes.

Heat oven to 400°. Bake until light brown, 13 to 15 minutes. 20 rolls.

CRESCENT ROLLS

Prepare Potato Refrigerator Dough (opposite). Divide into halves (refrigerate 1 half for future use or use for Parker House Rolls, above). Divide remaining half of dough into halves. Roll 1 half into 12-inch circle. Spread with margarine or butter, softened. Cut circle into 16 wedges. Roll up, beginning at rounded edges. Place rolls, with points underneath, on greased cookie sheet; curve ends slightly. Brush with margarine or butter, softened. Repeat with remaining dough. Let rise until double, 45 to 60 minutes.

Heat oven to 400°. Bake until light brown, 13 to 15 minutes. 32 rolls.

HAMBURGER BUNS

Divide ⅓ of Potato Refrigerator Dough (opposite) into 12 equal parts. Shape each part into smooth ball on lightly floured surface with lightly greased fingers; flatten. Place about 1 inch apart on greased cookie sheet. Let rise until double, 45 to 60 minutes.

Heat oven to 400°. Brush buns with margarine or butter, softened; sprinkle with sesame seed or poppy seed. Bake until golden brown, 13 to 15 minutes. 1 dozen rolls.

SQUASH ROLLS

1 cup milk	¼ cup warm water
2 tablespoons margarine	(105 to 115°)
or butter	1 cup mashed cooked
½ cup sugar	winter squash*
1 teaspoon salt	4½ to 5 cups Gold Medal
1 package active dry yeast	all-purpose flour**

Heat milk, margarine, sugar and salt until margarine is melted. Cool to lukewarm. Dissolve yeast in warm water in large mixing bowl. Stir in milk mixture, squash and 2 cups of the flour. Beat until smooth. Mix in enough remaining flour to make dough easy to handle.

Turn dough onto lightly floured surface; knead until smooth and elastic, about 5 minutes. Place in greased bowl; turn greased side up. Cover; let rise in warm place until double, about 1½ hours. (Dough is ready if indentation remains when touched.)

Punch down dough. Shape into 1-inch balls. Place 3 balls in each of 24 greased muffin cups, 2½ × 1¼ inches. Let rise until double, 30 to 45 minutes.

Heat oven to 400°. Bake until light brown, 15 to 20 minutes.

2 dozen rolls.

*1 cup frozen squash, thawed and brought to room temperature, can be substituted for the fresh squash.

**If using self-rising flour, omit salt.

HERB BUNS

1 package active dry yeast	2 tablespoons sugar
1 cup warm water	1 teaspoon salt
(105 to 115°)	1 egg
1 teaspoon caraway seed	2 tablespoons shortening
½ teaspoon dried sage	2¼ cups Gold Medal
leaves	all-purpose flour*
¼ teaspoon ground nutmeg	

Dissolve yeast in warm water in large mixing bowl. Add caraway seed, sage and nutmeg. Stir in sugar, salt, egg, shortening and 1 cup of the flour. Beat until smooth. Stir in remaining flour until smooth. Scrape batter from side of bowl. Cover; let rise in warm place until double, about 30 minutes.

Stir down batter by beating about 25 strokes. Spoon into 12 greased muffin cups, 2½ × 1¼ inches, filling each about half full. Let rise until batter reaches tops of cups, 20 to 30 minutes.

Heat oven to 400°. Bake 15 minutes. 1 dozen rolls.

*If using self-rising flour, omit salt.

Sour Cream-Chive Buns: Decrease warm water to ¼ cup. Omit caraway seed, sage and nutmeg. Mix ¾ cup dairy sour cream, the sugar, salt and shortening. Heat just to boiling; cool to lukewarm. Stir sour cream mixture and half of the flour into yeast. Beat until smooth. Mix in remaining flour, the egg and 1 tablespoon plus 1½ teaspoons snipped chives.

OVERNIGHT CARAMEL-PECAN ROLLS

2 packages active dry yeast	1 cup packed brown sugar
½ cup warm water (105 to 115°)	½ cup margarine or butter, softened
2 cups lukewarm milk (scalded then cooled)	2 tablespoons light corn syrup
⅓ cup granulated sugar	1 cup pecan halves
⅓ cup vegetable oil or shortening	4 tablespoons margarine or butter, softened
3 teaspoons baking powder	½ cup granulated sugar
2 teaspoons salt	1 tablespoon plus 1 teaspoon ground cinnamon
1 egg	
6½ to 7½ cups Gold Medal all-purpose flour*	

Dissolve yeast in warm water in large mixing bowl. Stir in milk, ⅓ cup sugar, the oil, baking powder, salt, egg and 3 cups of the flour. Beat until smooth. Mix in enough remaining flour to make dough easy to handle.

Turn dough onto well-floured surface; knead until smooth and elastic, 8 to 10 minutes. Place in greased bowl; turn greased side up. Cover; let rise in warm place until double, about 1½ hours. (Dough is ready if indentation remains when touched.)

Heat brown sugar and ½ cup margarine until melted; remove from heat. Stir in corn syrup. Divide mixture between 2 baking pans, 13×9×2 inches. Sprinkle each with ½ cup pecan halves.

Punch down dough; divide into halves. Roll 1 half into rectangle, 12×10 inches. Spread with 2 tablespoons of the margarine. Mix ½ cup sugar and the cinnamon; sprinkle half of the sugar mixture over rectangle. Roll up, beginning at 12-inch side. Pinch edge firmly to seal. Stretch roll to make even.

Cut roll into twelve 1-inch slices. Place slightly apart in 1 pan. Wrap pan tightly with heavy-duty aluminum foil. Repeat with remaining dough. Refrigerate at least 12 hours but no longer than 48 hours. (To bake immediately, do not wrap. Let rise in warm place until double, about 30 minutes. Bake as directed below.)

Heat oven to 350°. Remove foil from pans. Bake until golden, 30 to 35 minutes. Immediately invert pan on heatproof serving plate. Let pan remain a minute so caramel drizzles over rolls.

2 dozen rolls.

*If using self-rising flour, omit baking powder and salt.

Overnight Cinnamon Rolls: Omit caramel mixture; place slices in greased pans. Continue as directed. Mix 1 cup powdered sugar, 1 tablespoon milk and ½ teaspoon vanilla until smooth; spread over baked rolls (frosts 1 pan of rolls).

This is an updated version of the sticky buns so popular with 17th century Pennsylvania Dutch settlers. It calls for an overnight rising of the shaped rolls in the refrigerator ... an easy way to serve hot, homemade rolls for breakfast.

Orange Rolls

⑨ *range Rolls were featured in this company advertisement of 1939 as well as in* Betty Crocker's Picture Cook Book *of 1950. This recipe is among the company's oldest, dating back to the 1920s when the company first established a test kitchen.*

Lightly score top of roll at 1-inch intervals. Slip a 12-inch string under roll. Cross ends of string at each cut mark. Pull ends sharply through dough.

SWEET ROLL DOUGH

1 package active dry yeast
½ cup warm water
   (105 to 115°)
½ cup lukewarm milk
   (scalded then cooled)
⅓ cup sugar

⅓ cup shortening, or
   margarine or butter,
   softened
1 teaspoon salt
1 egg
3½ to 4 cups Gold Medal
   all-purpose flour*

Dissolve yeast in warm water in large mixing bowl. Stir in milk, sugar, shortening, salt, egg and 2 cups of the flour. Beat until smooth. Mix in enough remaining flour to make dough easy to handle.

Turn dough onto lightly floured surface; knead until smooth and elastic, about 5 minutes. Place in greased bowl; turn greased side up. (At this point, dough can be refrigerated 3 to 4 days.) Cover; let rise in warm place until double, about 1½ hours. (Dough is ready if indentation remains when touched.)

Punch down dough. Shape, let rise and bake as directed in the following recipes.

*If using self-rising flour, omit salt.

ORANGE ROLLS

1 cup powdered sugar
2 tablespoons margarine or
   butter, softened
2 teaspoons grated orange
   peel

1 tablespoon plus 1
   teaspoon orange juice
½ Sweet Roll Dough
   (above)

Beat powdered sugar, margarine, orange peel and orange juice until creamy. Roll dough into rectangle, 12×7 inches, on lightly floured surface; spread with half of the orange mixture. Roll up tightly, beginning at 12-inch side. Pinch edge firmly to seal. Stretch roll to make even. Cut into twelve 1-inch slices. Place slightly apart in greased round baking pan, 8×1½ inches. Let rise until double, about 40 minutes.

Heat oven to 375°. Bake until golden brown, 20 to 25 minutes. Frost with remaining orange mixture while warm.   1 dozen rolls.

CINNAMON TWISTS

½ recipe Sweet Roll Dough (opposite)
1 tablespoon margarine or butter, softened

3 tablespoons packed brown sugar
½ teaspoon ground cinnamon Creamy Glaze (below)

Roll dough into rectangle, 12×6 inches, on lightly floured surface; brush with margarine. Mix brown sugar and cinnamon; sprinkle lengthwise over half of the rectangle. Fold other half onto sugared half. Cut into twelve 1-inch strips.

Holding ends of each strip, twist in opposite directions. Place twists about 2 inches apart on greased cookie sheet; press ends of twists on cookie sheet. Cover; let rise until double, about 45 minutes.

Heat oven to 375°. Bake until golden brown, 12 to 15 minutes. Spread with Creamy Glaze while warm.   1 dozen rolls.

Creamy Glaze

Beat ¾ cup powdered sugar, 1 tablespoon margarine or butter, softened, ¾ teaspoon vanilla and 2 to 3 teaspoons hot water until smooth and of spreading consistency.

HUNGARIAN COFFEE CAKE

Sweet Roll Dough (opposite)
½ cup margarine or butter, melted

¾ cup sugar
1 teaspoon ground cinnamon
½ cup finely chopped nuts

Shape dough into 1½-inch balls. Dip into margarine, then into mixture of sugar, cinnamon and nuts. Place a single layer of balls in well-greased 10-inch tube pan so they just touch. (If pan has removable bottom, line with aluminum foil.) Top with another layer of balls. Let rise until double, about 40 minutes.

Heat oven to 375°. Bake until golden brown, 35 to 40 minutes. (If coffee cake is browning too quickly, cover with foil.) Loosen from pan. Immediately invert pan on heatproof serving plate. Let pan remain a minute so sugar mixture drizzles over coffee cake. To serve, break coffee cake apart with 2 forks.

23

HONEY-WHEAT TWIST

2	packages active dry yeast	1	egg
1	cup warm water (105 to 115°)	2¾	to 3 cups Gold Medal all-purpose flour*
¼	cup honey	¾	to 1 cup Gold Medal whole wheat flour
3	tablespoons margarine or butter, softened		Honey-Almond Glaze (below)
2	teaspoons salt		

Dissolve yeast in warm water in large bowl. Stir in honey, margarine, salt, egg and 2 cups all-purpose flour. Beat until smooth.

Divide dough into halves. Stir enough of the whole wheat flour into 1 half to form a soft dough. Stir enough of the remaining all-purpose flour into the other half to form a soft dough.

Turn each half onto lightly floured surface; knead until smooth and elastic, about 5 minutes. Place in greased bowls; turn greased sides up. Cover; let rise in warm place until double, about 1½ hours. (Dough is ready if indentation remains when touched.)

Punch down dough; roll each half into rope, about 15 inches long. Place ropes side by side on greased cookie sheet; twist together gently and loosely. Pinch ends to fasten. Let rise until double, about 1 hour.

Heat oven to 350°. Bake until twist is golden brown and sounds hollow when tapped, 30 to 35 minutes. Remove from sheet; cool slightly on wire rack. Spread with Honey-Almond Glaze.

*If using self-rising flour, omit salt.

Honey-Almond Glaze

Cook and stir ¼ cup chopped almonds and 1 tablespoon margarine or butter until almonds are brown. Stir in ¼ cup honey and 2 tablespoons sugar. Heat to boiling, stirring constantly; cool.

This picture puzzle contest appeared in a Gold Medal advertisement in the Saturday Evening Post in 1921. Nearly 30,000 people sent in correct solutions, along with an avalanche of consumer mail requesting recipes and asking about baking problems. Company officials decided their responses should be signed with a woman's name. The name selected was Betty Crocker ... Betty, because it was a familiar, friendly name and Crocker, to honor a popular company director, William C. Crocker.

APRICOT CREAM CAKE

Roll ⅓ of Potato Refrigerator Dough (page 18) into 15-inch circle; place over greased 9-inch ring mold. Fit dough into ring mold (outer edge of circle will come to rim of mold). Spoon Cream Cheese Filling (below) onto dough. Lap edge of circle over filling; seal to inside ring of dough. Cut a cross in dough that covers the center of the mold. Fold each triangle formed back over ring and pinch each point to dough to seal securely. Let rise until double, about 1½ hours.

Heat oven to 350°. Bake about 30 minutes. Remove cake from pan. Place cake, top side up, on serving plate. Heat ½ cup apricot jam until melted; spoon onto ring. Sprinkle with 1 tablespoon powdered sugar.

Cream Cheese Filling

1 package (8 ounces) cream cheese, softened	1 egg yolk
¼ cup sugar	½ teaspoon grated lemon peel
3 tablespoons Gold Medal all-purpose flour	1 tablespoon lemon juice

Beat cream cheese and sugar until light and fluffy. Stir in remaining ingredients.

Fold edge of dough over filling. Seal edge to inside of ring.

BAKING POWDER BISCUITS

⅓	cup shortening	2½	teaspoons baking
1¾	cups Gold Medal		powder
	all-purpose flour*	¾	teaspoon salt
		¾	cup milk

Heat oven to 450°. Cut shortening into flour, baking powder and salt with pastry blender until mixture resembles fine crumbs. Stir in just enough milk so dough leaves side of bowl and rounds up into a ball. (Too much milk makes dough sticky; not enough milk makes biscuits dry.)

Turn dough onto lightly floured surface. Knead lightly 10 times. Roll or pat ½ inch thick. Cut with floured 2-inch biscuit cutter. Place on ungreased cookie sheet about 1 inch apart for crusty sides, touching for soft sides. Bake until golden brown, 10 to 12 minutes. Immediately remove from cookie sheet.

About 1 dozen biscuits.

*If using self-rising flour, omit baking powder and salt.

Biscuit Sticks: Heat ⅓ cup margarine or butter in baking pan, 9×9×2 inches, in oven until melted; remove from oven. Roll dough into 8-inch square. Cut dough into halves; cut each half into eight 1-inch strips. Dip strips into margarine, coating all sides. Arrange strips in 2 rows in pan. Bake until golden brown, about 15 minutes.   16 sticks.

26

BLUEBERRY MUFFINS

1 egg	3 teaspoons baking powder
1 cup milk	1 teaspoon salt
¼ cup vegetable oil	1 cup fresh blueberries or ¾
2 cups Gold Medal	cup well-drained frozen
all-purpose flour*	(thawed) blueberries
¼ cup sugar	

Heat oven to 400°. Grease bottoms only of 12 muffin cups, 2½×1¼ inches. Beat egg; stir in milk and oil. Mix in flour, sugar, baking powder and salt just until flour is moistened (batter will be lumpy). Fold in blueberries. Fill muffin cups ⅔ full. Bake until golden brown, 20 to 25 minutes. Immediately remove from pan.
1 dozen muffins.

*If using self-rising flour, omit baking powder and salt.

Cranberry-Orange Muffins: Omit blueberries. Fold 1 tablespoon grated orange peel and 1 cup cranberries, cut into halves, into batter.

During the early 1930s, Gold Medal advertisements featured winning recipes from state fair competitions across the country. This Blueberry Muffin recipe took top prize at the Illinois State Fair.

FRENCH BREAKFAST PUFFS

⅓ cup shortening	¼ teaspoon ground nutmeg
½ cup sugar	½ cup milk
1 egg	½ cup sugar
1½ cups Gold Medal	1 teaspoon ground
all-purpose flour*	cinnamon
1½ teaspoons baking	½ cup margarine or butter,
powder	melted
½ teaspoon salt	

Heat oven to 350°. Grease 15 muffin cups, 2½×1¼ inches. Mix shortening, ½ cup sugar and the egg. Stir in flour, baking powder, salt and nutmeg alternately with milk. Fill muffin cups about ⅔ full. Bake until golden brown, 20 to 25 minutes. Mix ½ cup sugar and the cinnamon. Immediately after baking, roll puffs in melted margarine, then in sugar-cinnamon mixture. 15 puffs.

*If using self-rising flour, omit baking powder and salt.

℘A Colonial favorite, Steamed Brown Bread appeared in many Gold Medal cookbooks, beginning with <u>Miss Parloa's New Cook Book</u> of 1880.

APPLE-RAISIN BREAD

3 cups chopped unpared apples	2 teaspoons ground cinnamon
3 cups Gold Medal all-purpose flour*	1½ teaspoons salt
2½ cups sugar	1½ teaspoons baking soda
1¼ cups vegetable oil	1 teaspoon ground cloves
4 eggs, beaten	½ teaspoon baking powder
1 tablespoon plus 1 teaspoon vanilla	⅔ cup raisins
	½ cup chopped nuts

Heat oven to 325°. Generously grease bottoms only of 2 baking pans, 9×5×3 inches. Beat all ingredients on low speed, scraping bowl constantly, 1 minute. Beat on medium speed 1 minute. Pour into pans. Bake until wooden pick inserted in center comes out clean, about 1 hour. Cool 10 minutes; remove from pans. Cool completely before slicing. Store in refrigerator.   2 loaves.

*If using self-rising flour, omit salt, baking soda and baking powder.

Zucchini Bread: Substitute 4 cups coarsely shredded zucchini for the apples (do not shred in blender). Omit raisins and increase nuts to 1 cup.

STEAMED BROWN BREAD

2 cups buttermilk	1 cup raisins, if desired
1 cup Gold Medal all-purpose flour*	¾ cup light or dark molasses
1 cup cornmeal	2 teaspoons baking soda
1 cup Gold Medal whole wheat flour	1 teaspoon salt

Grease four 16-ounce vegetable cans (4¼×3 inches) or 7-inch tube mold. Beat all ingredients in large mixer bowl on low speed, scraping bowl constantly, 30 seconds. Beat on medium speed, scraping bowl constantly, 30 seconds. Fill cans about ⅔ full. Cover tightly with aluminum foil.

Place cans on rack in Dutch oven or steamer; pour boiling water into Dutch oven to level of rack. Cover Dutch oven. Keep water boiling over low heat until wooden pick inserted in center comes out clean, about 3 hours. (Add boiling water during steaming if necessary.) Immediately unmold bread.   4 loaves.

*If using self-rising flour, decrease baking soda to 1 teaspoon and omit salt.

Baked Brown Bread: Heat oven to 325°. Pour batter into greased 2-quart round casserole. Bake about 1 hour.

Place wire rack in Dutch oven; place covered cans on rack. Fill boiling water to level of rack.

Loosen sides of bread with spatula. Unmold bread on wire rack.

NUT BREAD

2½ cups Gold Medal all-purpose flour*	2 eggs
1¼ cups buttermilk**	3 teaspoons baking powder
½ cup granulated sugar	1 teaspoon salt
½ cup packed brown sugar	½ teaspoon baking soda
¼ cup shortening	1 cup chopped nuts

Heat oven to 350°. Grease and flour baking pan, 9×5×3 inches. Beat all ingredients in large mixer bowl on low speed 15 seconds. Beat on medium speed, scraping bowl constantly, 30 seconds. Pour into pan. Bake until wooden pick inserted in center comes out clean, 60 to 65 minutes. Immediately remove from pan; cool completely. Store at least 8 hours before slicing.

*If using self-rising flour, omit baking powder, salt and baking soda and substitute whole milk for the buttermilk.

**To substitute soured milk for the buttermilk, add 1¼ cups whole milk to 1 tablespoon vinegar. Let stand 5 minutes. Use with all-purpose flour only.

Cherry-Nut Bread: Decrease buttermilk to 1 cup and add ¼ cup maraschino cherry juice. After beating, stir in ½ cup chopped drained maraschino cherries. Bake 70 to 75 minutes.

Date-Nut Bread: Omit buttermilk. Add 1½ cups boiling water to 1½ cups cut-up dates; stir and let cool. Beat in date mixture with the flour. Bake 65 to 70 minutes.

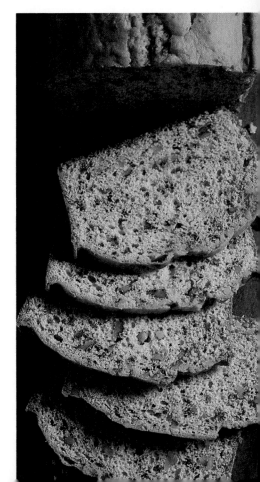

CAKE DOUGHNUTS

Vegetable oil
3⅓ cups Gold Medal all-purpose flour*
1 cup sugar
3 teaspoons baking powder
½ teaspoon salt
½ teaspoon ground cinnamon
¼ teaspoon ground nutmeg
2 tablespoons shortening
2 eggs
¾ cup milk
Chocolate Glaze or Browned Butter Glaze (below)

Heat oil (2 to 3 inches) in deep-fat fryer or heavy kettle to 375°. Beat 1½ cups of the flour and the remaining ingredients except glaze in large mixer bowl on low speed, scraping bowl constantly, 30 seconds. Beat on medium speed, scraping bowl occasionally, 2 minutes. Stir in remaining flour.

Turn half of the dough onto well-floured cloth-covered board; roll around lightly to coat with flour. Roll gently ⅜ inch thick. Cut with floured doughnut cutter. Repeat with remaining dough.

Slide doughnuts into hot oil with wide spatula. Turn doughnuts as they rise to surface. Fry until golden brown, 1 to 1½ minutes on each side. Remove from oil; do not prick doughnuts. Drain on paper towels. Spread doughnuts with Chocolate Glaze. Sprinkle with flaked coconut, chopped nuts or decors if desired.

2 dozen doughnuts.

*If using self-rising flour, omit baking powder and salt.

Chocolate Glaze

Mix 2½ cups powdered sugar, 1 ounce melted unsweetened chocolate (cool) and ½ teaspoon vanilla. Gradually beat in about ¼ cup milk until smooth and of desired consistency.

Browned Butter Glaze

Heat ¼ cup margarine or butter over low heat until delicate brown; remove from heat. Mix in 2½ cups powdered sugar. Beat in 1 teaspoon vanilla and 2 to 3 tablespoons milk until smooth and of desired consistency.

Applesauce Doughnuts: Decrease sugar to ¾ cup and add 1 cup applesauce. Omit cinnamon and milk. Increase nutmeg to ¾ teaspoon and add ¼ teaspoon ground cloves. Cover and refrigerate dough until stiff, about 1 hour. Continue as directed. Spread doughnuts with Browned Butter Glaze.

DANISH PUFF

½ cup butter, softened
1 cup Gold Medal
    all-purpose flour*
2 tablespoons water
½ cup butter
1 cup water
1 teaspoon almond extract

1 cup Gold Medal
    all-purpose flour*
3 eggs
    Powdered Sugar Glaze
    (below)
    Chopped nuts

Heat oven to 350°. Cut ½ cup butter into 1 cup flour until particles are size of small peas. Sprinkle 2 tablespoons water over flour mixture; mix with fork. Gather pastry into a ball; divide into halves. Pat each half into rectangle, 12×3 inches, on ungreased cookie sheet. Rectangles should be about 3 inches apart.

Heat ½ cup butter and 1 cup water to rolling boil; remove from heat. Quickly stir in almond extract and 1 cup flour. Stir vigorously over low heat until mixture forms a ball, about 1 minute; remove from heat. Add eggs; beat until smooth and glossy. Spread half of the topping over each rectangle. Bake until topping is crisp and brown, about 1 hour; cool. (Topping will shrink and fall, forming the custardy top.) Spread with Powdered Sugar Glaze; sprinkle with nuts.

                    2 coffee cakes (5 or 6 servings each).

*Self-rising flour can be used in this recipe.

Powdered Sugar Glaze

Mix 1½ cups powdered sugar, 2 tablespoons margarine or butter, softened, and 1½ teaspoons vanilla. Stir in 1 to 2 tablespoons warm water, 1 teaspoon at a time, until smooth and of desired consistency.

Pat each half of dough into rectangle on ungreased cookie sheet.

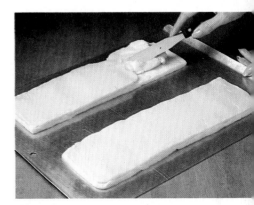

Spread custardy topping over each unbaked rectangle.

SOUR CREAM COFFEE CAKE

1½ cups sugar	1½ teaspoons baking
¾ cup margarine or butter, softened	powder
	1½ teaspoons baking soda
3 eggs	¾ teaspoon salt
1½ teaspoons vanilla	1½ cups dairy sour cream
3 cups Gold Medal all-purpose* or whole wheat flour	Filling (below)
	Light Brown Glaze (below)

Heat oven to 350°. Grease tube pan, 10×4 inches, 12-cup bundt cake pan or 2 baking pans, 9×5×3 inches. Beat sugar, margarine, eggs and vanilla in large mixer bowl on medium speed, scraping bowl occasionally, 2 minutes. Beat in flour, baking powder, baking soda and salt alternately with sour cream on low speed. Prepare Filling.

For tube or bundt cake pan, spread ⅓ of the batter (about 2 cups) in pan and sprinkle with ⅓ of the Filling (about 6 tablespoons); repeat 2 times. For loaf pans, spread ¼ of the batter (about 1½ cups) in each pan and sprinkle each with ¼ of the Filling (about 5 tablespoons); repeat.

Bake until wooden pick inserted near center comes out clean, about 1 hour. Cool slightly; remove from pan(s). Cool 10 minutes; drizzle with Light Brown Glaze.   14 to 16 servings.

*If using self-rising flour, omit baking powder, baking soda and salt.

Filling

Mix ½ cup packed brown sugar, ½ cup finely chopped nuts and 1½ teaspoons ground cinnamon.

Light Brown Glaze

Heat ¼ cup margarine or butter in 1½-quart saucepan over medium heat until delicate brown. Stir in 2 cups powdered sugar and 1 teaspoon vanilla. Stir in 1 to 2 tablespoons milk, 1 tablespoon at a time, until smooth and of desired consistency.

In 1924 Washburn Crosby Company produced radio's first consumer food service program...the Betty Crocker "Cooking School of the Air." It continued without interruption for 24 years, attracting more than 1 million formal registrations by homemaker listeners.

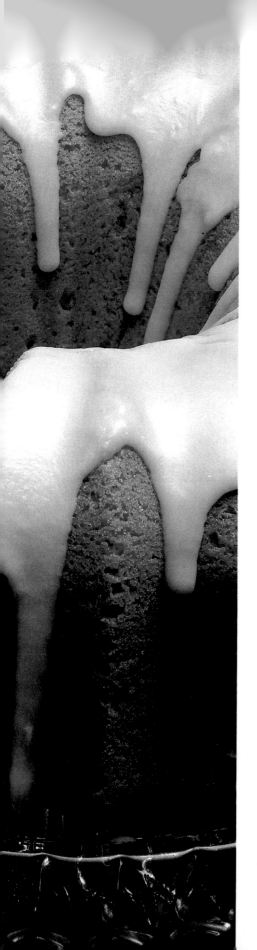

FRUIT SWIRL COFFEE CAKE

1½	cups sugar	4	eggs
½	cup margarine or butter, softened	3	cups Gold Medal all-purpose flour*
½	cup shortening	1	can (21 ounces) apricot, blueberry or cherry pie filling
1½	teaspoons baking powder		Glaze (below)
1	teaspoon vanilla		
1	teaspoon almond extract		

Heat oven to 350°. Grease jelly roll pan, 15½×10½ ×1 inch, or 2 baking pans, 9×9×2 inches. Beat sugar, margarine, shortening, baking powder, vanilla, almond extract and eggs in large mixer bowl on low speed, scraping bowl constantly, until blended. Beat on high speed, scraping bowl occasionally, 3 minutes. Stir in flour. Spread ⅔ of the batter in jelly roll pan or ⅓ in each square pan. Spread pie filling over batter. Drop remaining batter by tablespoonfuls onto pie filling.

Bake until light brown, about 45 minutes. Drizzle with Glaze while warm. Cut cake in jelly roll pan into bars, about 2½×2 inches; cut cake in square pans into about 2¾-inch squares.

30 bars or 18 squares.

*If using self-rising flour, omit baking powder.

Glaze

Beat 1 cup powdered sugar and 1 to 2 tablespoons milk until smooth and of desired consistency.

Cookies

BROWNIES

4 squares (1 ounce each) unsweetened chocolate
⅔ cup shortening
2 cups sugar
4 eggs
1 teaspoon vanilla

1¼ cups Gold Medal all-purpose flour*
1 teaspoon baking powder
1 teaspoon salt
1 cup chopped nuts, if desired

Heat oven to 350°. Grease baking pan, 13×9×2 inches. Heat chocolate and shortening in 3-quart saucepan over low heat until melted; remove from heat. Stir in sugar, eggs and vanilla. Mix in remaining ingredients. Spread in pan. Bake until brownies begin to pull away from sides of pan, about 30 minutes. (Do not overbake.) Cool slightly; spread with Glossy Chocolate Frosting (below) if desired. Cool completely; cut into bars, about 2×1½ inches.

3 dozen cookies.

*If using self-rising flour, omit baking powder and salt.

Glossy Chocolate Frosting

3 squares (1 ounce each) unsweetened chocolate
3 tablespoons shortening
2 cups powdered sugar
¼ teaspoon salt

⅓ cup milk
1 teaspoon vanilla
½ cup finely chopped nuts, if desired

Heat chocolate and shortening over low heat until melted. Stir in powdered sugar, salt, milk and vanilla; beat until smooth. Place pan of frosting in bowl of ice and water; continue beating until smooth and of spreading consistency. Stir in nuts.

OATMEAL BROWNIES

2½ cups quick-cooking or regular oats
¾ cup Gold Medal all-purpose flour
¾ cup packed brown sugar

½ teaspoon baking soda
¾ cup margarine or butter, melted
Brownies (above)

Heat oven to 350°. Grease baking pan, 13×9×2 inches. Mix oats, flour, brown sugar and baking soda; stir in margarine. Reserve ¾ cup of the oatmeal mixture. Press remaining oatmeal mixture in pan. Bake 10 minutes; cool 5 minutes.

Prepare Brownies as directed except — omit nuts. Spread dough over baked layer. Sprinkle with reserved oatmeal mixture. Bake until brownies begin to pull away from sides of pan, about 35 minutes. (Do not overbake.) Cool; cut into about 1½-inch squares.

4 dozen cookies.

Brownies, top, became popular in the 1920s. Oatmeal Brownies, bottom, were featured in the Gold Medal recipe collection of 1925. Some say brownies were originally a fallen chocolate cake. Others believe brownies are an American version of Scottish cocoa scones. Whatever the origin, the first brownies in the U.S. were called Bangor Brownies after the city in Maine where they were discovered.

CHOCOLATE CHIP BARS

½ cup granulated sugar
⅓ cup packed brown sugar
½ cup margarine or butter, softened
1 teaspoon vanilla
1 egg

1¼ cups Gold Medal all-purpose flour
½ teaspoon baking soda
½ teaspoon salt
½ cup chopped nuts
1 package (6 ounces) semi-sweet chocolate chips

Heat oven to 375°. Grease and flour baking pan, 13×9×2 inches. Mix sugars, margarine and vanilla. Beat in egg. Stir in flour, baking soda and salt. Mix in nuts and chocolate chips. Spread dough in pan. Bake until light brown, 12 to 14 minutes. Cool; cut into bars, about 2×1½ inches.   3 dozen cookies.

Peanut Butter-Chocolate Chip Bars: Decrease margarine to ¼ cup and mix in ⅓ cup peanut butter. Beat in 2 tablespoons water with the egg. Use ½ cup chopped peanuts. Bake 22 to 25 minutes.

LEMON SQUARES

1 cup Gold Medal all-purpose flour*	2 teaspoons grated lemon peel, if desired
½ cup margarine or butter, softened	2 tablespoons lemon juice
¼ cup powdered sugar	½ teaspoon baking powder
1 cup granulated sugar	¼ teaspoon salt
2 eggs	Powdered sugar

Heat oven to 350°. Mix flour, margarine and ¼ cup powdered sugar. Press in ungreased baking pan, 8×8×2 inches, building up ½-inch edges. Bake 20 minutes.

Beat granulated sugar, eggs, lemon peel, lemon juice, baking powder and salt until light and fluffy, about 3 minutes; pour over baked layer. Bake just until no indentation remains when touched in center, about 25 minutes. Cool; sprinkle with powdered sugar. Cut into about 1-inch squares.   64 cookies.

*If using self-rising flour, omit baking powder and salt.

COCONUT-TOFFEE BARS

½ cup packed brown sugar	1 cup Gold Medal all-purpose flour*
¼ cup margarine or butter, softened	Coconut-Almond Topping (below)
¼ cup shortening	

Heat oven to 350°. Mix brown sugar, margarine and shortening. Stir in flour. Press in ungreased baking pan, 13×9×2 inches. Bake 10 minutes.

Spread Coconut-Almond Topping over baked layer. Bake until golden brown, about 25 minutes. Cool slightly; cut into bars, about 3×1 inch.   3 dozen cookies.

Coconut-Almond Topping

2 eggs	1 teaspoon vanilla
1 cup packed brown sugar	½ teaspoon salt
2 tablespoons Gold Medal all-purpose flour*	1 cup shredded coconut
1 teaspoon baking powder	1 cup chopped almonds

Beat eggs; stir in remaining ingredients.

*Self-rising flour can be used in this recipe; omit baking powder and salt from topping.

Coconut-Toffee Bars won raves from Gold Medal users, and a packaged mix was developed using these bar cookies as the model.

SOUR CREAM-BANANA BARS

1½ cups sugar
1 cup dairy sour cream
½ cup margarine or butter, softened
2 eggs
1½ cups mashed bananas (about 3 large)
2 teaspoons vanilla

2 cups Gold Medal all-purpose flour
1 teaspoon salt
1 teaspoon baking soda
½ cup chopped nuts
Browned Butter Frosting (below)

Heat oven to 375°. Grease and flour jelly roll pan, 15½ × 10½ × 1 inch. Mix sugar, sour cream, margarine and eggs in large mixer bowl on low speed, scraping bowl occasionally, 1 minute. Beat in bananas and vanilla on low speed 30 seconds. Beat in flour, salt and baking soda on medium speed, scraping bowl occasionally, 1 minute. Stir in nuts. Spread dough in pan. Bake until light brown, 20 to 25 minutes. Cool; frost with Browned Butter Frosting. Cut into bars, about 2 × 1½ inches.   4 dozen cookies.

Browned Butter Frosting

Heat ¼ cup margarine or butter over medium heat until delicate brown; remove from heat. Mix in 2 cups powdered sugar. Beat in 1 teaspoon vanilla and 3 tablespoons milk until smooth and of spreading consistency.

PUMPKIN-SPICE BARS

4 eggs
2 cups sugar
1 cup vegetable oil
1 can (16 ounces) pumpkin
2 cups Gold Medal all-purpose flour
2 teaspoons baking powder
2 teaspoons ground cinnamon

1 teaspoon baking soda
¾ teaspoon salt
½ teaspoon ground ginger
¼ teaspoon ground cloves
½ cup raisins
Cream Cheese Frosting (below)
½ cup chopped nuts

Heat oven to 350°. Grease jelly roll pan, 15½ × 10½ × 1 inch. Beat eggs, sugar, oil and pumpkin. Stir in flour, baking powder, cinnamon, baking soda, salt, ginger and cloves. Mix in raisins. Pour batter into pan. Bake until light brown, 25 to 30 minutes. Cool; frost with Cream Cheese Frosting. Sprinkle with nuts. Cut into bars, about 2 × 1½ inches. Refrigerate any remaining bars.
49 cookies.

Cream Cheese Frosting

Mix 1 package (3 ounces) cream cheese, softened, ¼ cup plus 2 tablespoons margarine or butter, softened, and 1 teaspoon vanilla. Gradually beat in 2 cups powdered sugar until smooth and of spreading consistency.

Left, Applesauce Jumbles; Top, Ginger Creams; Bottom, Hermits

ℋermits originated in Cape Cod during the days of the Clipper Ships. They kept well when stored in canisters aboard ship on long sea voyages. A Washburn Crosby cookbook of the late 1800s noted in a recipe for Hermits that the raisins, a traditional ingredient, must be "stoned and chopped."

HERMITS

1 cup packed brown sugar	½ teaspoon ground nutmeg
¼ cup margarine or butter, softened	1¾ cups Gold Medal all-purpose flour*
¼ cup shortening	½ teaspoon baking soda
¼ cup cold coffee	½ teaspoon salt
1 egg	1¼ cups raisins
½ teaspoon ground cinnamon	¾ cup chopped nuts

Heat oven to 375°. Mix brown sugar, margarine, shortening, coffee, egg, cinnamon and nutmeg. Stir in remaining ingredients. Drop dough by rounded teaspoonfuls about 2 inches apart onto ungreased cookie sheet. Bake until almost no indentation remains when touched, 8 to 10 minutes. Immediately remove from cookie sheet.   About 4 dozen cookies.

*If using self-rising flour, omit baking soda and salt.

APPLESAUCE JUMBLES

2¾	cups Gold Medal all-purpose flour*	1	teaspoon ground cinnamon
1½	cups packed brown sugar	1	teaspoon vanilla
1	teaspoon salt	¼	teaspoon ground cloves
½	teaspoon baking soda	1	cup raisins
¾	cup applesauce	1	cup chopped nuts, if desired
½	cup shortening		Browned Butter Glaze (below)
2	eggs		

Mix all ingredients except glaze. (If dough is soft, cover and refrigerate.) Heat oven to 375°. Drop dough by rounded tea-spoonfuls about 2 inches apart onto ungreased cookie sheet. Bake until almost no indentation remains when touched, about 10 minutes. Immediately remove from cookie sheet. Cool; spread with Browned Butter Glaze.   4½ to 5 dozen cookies.

*If using self-rising flour, omit salt and baking soda.

Browned Butter Glaze

Heat ⅓ cup margarine or butter over low heat until golden brown; remove from heat. Stir in 2 cups powdered sugar and 1½ teaspoons vanilla. Beat in 2 to 4 tablespoons hot water until smooth and of desired consistency.

*J*umbles appeared on the scene as early as Colonial days. Over the years, homemakers have created many delightful variations on the basic recipe. There were Bedford Jumbles, Philadelphia Jumbles, Coconut Jumbles and even Wine Jumbles. The first Washburn Crosby cookbook offered a rolled version of today's drop-style Jumbles. Some Jumbles recipes included sour cream or butter-milk. Dates, raisins, grated lemon, nutmeg, ginger and cin-namon all have been used as in-gredients. During the depression era and World War II, Jumbles recipes replaced much of the sugar with molasses and reduced the amount of shortening.

GINGER CREAMS

½	cup sugar	½	teaspoon salt
⅓	cup shortening	½	teaspoon baking soda
1	egg	½	teaspoon ground nutmeg
½	cup light or dark molasses	½	teaspoon ground cloves
½	cup water	½	teaspoon ground cinnamon
2	cups Gold Medal all-purpose flour*		Vanilla Butter Frosting (below)
1	teaspoon ground ginger		

Mix sugar, shortening, egg, molasses and water. Stir in remaining ingredients except frosting. Cover and refrigerate at least 1 hour.

Heat oven to 400°. Drop dough by rounded teaspoonfuls about 2 inches apart onto ungreased cookie sheet. Bake until almost no indentation remains when touched, about 8 minutes. Immediate-ly remove from cookie sheet. Cool; frost with Vanilla Butter Frosting.
                    About 4 dozen cookies.

*If using self-rising flour, omit salt and baking soda.

Vanilla Butter Frosting

Mix ¼ cup margarine or butter, softened, and 2 cups powdered sugar. Beat in about 1 tablespoon milk and 1 teaspoon vanilla until smooth and of spreading consistency.

*G*inger Creams feature the flavor combination so popular with Gold Medal users during the early 1900s. Molasses plus ginger, nutmeg, cinnamon and cloves created a rich, mellow taste that was more spicy than sweet. The cookies were frosted with vanilla or lemon frosting.

Chocolate chip cookies date back to The Depression Era when Ruth Wakefield of the Toll House Inn in Whitman, Massachusetts, chopped a bar of leftover semisweet chocolate and added the bits to dough for Butter Drop Cookies, a basic cookie recipe from Colonial America. A visitor at the Inn that day tasted the cookies and described them later to a friend who worked for a Boston newspaper, and Toll House cookies with their little chips of chocolate made the news. In 1940 chocolate chip cookies were introduced to homemakers on the Betty Crocker coast to coast radio series, "Famous Foods from Famous Places."

CHOCOLATE CHIP COOKIES

½ cup granulated sugar	1½ cups Gold Medal
½ cup packed brown sugar	all-purpose flour*
⅓ cup margarine or butter,	½ teaspoon baking soda
softened	½ teaspoon salt
⅓ cup shortening	½ cup chopped nuts
1 egg	1 package (6 ounces) semi-
1 teaspoon vanilla	sweet chocolate chips

Heat oven to 375°. Mix sugars, margarine, shortening, egg and vanilla. Stir in remaining ingredients. Drop dough by rounded teaspoonfuls about 2 inches apart onto ungreased cookie sheet. Bake until light brown, 8 to 10 minutes. Cool slightly before removing from cookie sheet.   About 3½ dozen cookies.

*If using self-rising flour, omit baking soda and salt.

HONEY-OATMEAL COOKIES

1¼ cups sugar	1 teaspoon baking soda
½ cup shortening	1 teaspoon salt
2 eggs	2 cups quick-cooking or
⅓ cup honey	regular oats
1¾ cups Gold Medal	1 cup raisins
all-purpose flour*	½ cup chopped nuts

Heat oven to 375°. Mix sugar, shortening, eggs and honey. Stir in remaining ingredients. Drop dough by rounded teaspoonfuls about 2 inches apart onto ungreased cookie sheet. Bake until light brown, 8 to 10 minutes. Immediately remove from cookie sheet.
                    About 5 dozen cookies.

*If using self-rising flour, omit baking soda and salt.

Left to right; Chocolate Chip Cookies, Honey-Oatmeal Cookies, Chocolate Drop Cookies

CHOCOLATE DROP COOKIES

1 cup sugar	1¾ cups Gold Medal all-purpose flour*
½ cup margarine or butter, softened	½ teaspoon baking soda
1 egg	½ teaspoon salt
2 ounces melted unsweetened chocolate (cool)	1 cup chopped nuts, if desired
⅓ cup buttermilk or water	Chocolate Frosting (below)
1 teaspoon vanilla	

Heat oven to 400°. Mix sugar, margarine, egg, chocolate, buttermilk and vanilla. Stir in flour, baking soda, salt and nuts. Drop dough by rounded teaspoonfuls about 2 inches apart onto ungreased cookie sheet. Bake until almost no indentation remains when touched, 8 to 10 minutes. Immediately remove from cookie sheet. Cool; frost with Chocolate Frosting.

About 4½ dozen cookies.

*If using self-rising flour, omit baking soda and salt.

Chocolate Frosting

Heat 2 squares (1 ounce each) unsweetened chocolate and 2 tablespoons margarine or butter over low heat until melted; remove from heat. Beat in 3 tablespoons water and about 2 cups powdered sugar until smooth and of spreading consistency.

*T*he Gold Medal Flour Home Service Recipe Box was introduced in 1925 to replace the popular *Gold Medal Flour Cook Book* which had been in print since 1903. The little oak recipe box — filled with recipes — was sold to consumers for $1. From 1925 to 1935, more than 350,000 of these boxes were distributed.

SALTED PEANUT CRISPS

1½ cups packed brown sugar
½ cup margarine or butter, softened
½ cup shortening
2 eggs
2 teaspoons vanilla

3 cups Gold Medal all-purpose flour*
½ teaspoon salt
½ teaspoon baking soda
2 cups salted peanuts

Heat oven to 375°. Mix brown sugar, margarine, shortening, eggs and vanilla. Stir in remaining ingredients. Drop dough by rounded teaspoonfuls about 2 inches apart onto lightly greased cookie sheet. Flatten with greased bottom of glass dipped in sugar. Bake until golden brown, 8 to 10 minutes. Immediately remove from cookie sheet.   About 6 dozen cookies.

*If using self-rising flour, omit salt and baking soda.

CHOCOLATE CRINKLES

2 cups granulated sugar
½ cup vegetable oil
4 ounces melted unsweetened chocolate (cool)
2 teaspoons vanilla
4 eggs

2 cups Gold Medal all-purpose flour*
2 teaspoons baking powder
½ teaspoon salt
½ cup powdered sugar

Mix granulated sugar, oil, chocolate and vanilla. Mix in eggs, 1 at a time. Stir in flour, baking powder and salt. Cover and refrigerate at least 3 hours.

Heat oven to 350°. Shape dough by rounded teaspoonfuls into balls. Roll in powdered sugar. Place about 2 inches apart on greased cookie sheet. Bake until almost no indentation remains when touched, 10 to 12 minutes.   About 6 dozen cookies.

*If using self-rising flour, omit baking powder and salt.

SNICKERDOODLES

1½ cups sugar
½ cup margarine or butter, softened
½ cup shortening
2 eggs
2¾ cups Gold Medal all-purpose flour*

2 teaspoons cream of tartar
1 teaspoon baking soda
¼ teaspoon salt
2 tablespoons sugar
2 teaspoons ground cinnamon

Heat oven to 400°. Mix 1½ cups sugar, the margarine, shortening and eggs. Stir in flour, cream of tartar, baking soda and salt. Shape dough by rounded teaspoonfuls into balls. Mix 2 tablespoons sugar and the cinnamon; roll balls in mixture to coat. Place about 2 inches apart on ungreased cookie sheet. Bake until set, 8 to 10 minutes. Immediately remove from cookie sheet.
                 About 6 dozen cookies.

*If using self-rising flour, omit cream of tartar, baking soda and salt.

Bonbon Cookies were created in 1955 when candy-like cookies were in vogue. The headline on a Gold Medal flour advertisement featuring the cookies said, "Bake as cookies. Eat as candy."

BONBON COOKIES

¾ cup powdered sugar
½ cup margarine or butter, softened
1 tablespoon vanilla
Few drops food color, if desired
1½ cups Gold Medal all-purpose flour*

⅛ teaspoon salt
Dates, nuts, semisweet chocolate chips, candied cherries or maraschino cherries
Glaze (below)

Heat oven to 350°. Mix powdered sugar, margarine, vanilla and food color. Work in flour and salt until dough holds together. (If dough is dry, mix in 1 to 2 tablespoons milk.) For each cookie, shape dough by tablespoonful around date, nut, chocolate chips or cherry to form ball. Place about 1 inch apart on ungreased cookie sheet. Bake until set but not brown, 12 to 15 minutes. Cool; dip tops of cookies into Glaze. Decorate with coconut, nuts, colored sugar, chocolate chips or chocolate shot if desired.

About 2 dozen cookies.

*Do not use self-rising flour in this recipe.

Glaze

Beat 1 cup powdered sugar, 1 tablespoon plus 1½ teaspoons milk and 1 teaspoon vanilla until smooth and of desired consistency. Tint with few drops food color if desired.

Shape about 1 tablespoonful of dough around nut. Place on ungreased cookie sheet.

Dip tops of cookies in Glaze. Place on wire rack. Decorate with coconut, nuts, colored sugar, chocolate chips or chocolate shot.

45

SUGAR COOKIES

1 cup sugar	1 teaspoon vanilla or ½
¾ cup shortening (part	teaspoon lemon extract
margarine or butter,	2½ cups Gold Medal
softened)	all-purpose flour*
2 eggs	1 teaspoon baking powder
	1 teaspoon salt

Mix sugar, shortening, eggs and vanilla. Stir in remaining ingredients. Cover and refrigerate at least 1 hour.

Heat oven to 400°. Roll dough ⅛ inch thick on lightly floured cloth-covered board. Cut into desired shapes with 3-inch cookie cutters. Place on ungreased cookie sheet. Bake until very light brown, 6 to 8 minutes.   About 4 dozen cookies.

*If using self-rising flour, omit baking powder and salt.

Hand Cookies: Roll dough 3/16 inch thick. Place hand lightly on dough; trace around hand with pastry wheel. Bake until no indentation remains when touched, 6 to 8 minutes. Cool; decorate as desired.   About 15 cookies.

FILLED SUGAR COOKIES

Prepare dough for Sugar Cookies (above). Cover and refrigerate at least 1 hour.

Heat oven to 400°. Cut dough into 48 rounds with doughnut cutter that has center removed. Cut out centers of 24 of the rounds with center of doughnut cutter. Place uncut rounds on lightly greased cookie sheet. Top with Raisin Filling or Cherry-Apricot Filling (below), spreading almost to edges. Top with remaining rounds. Press edges together with fingers or floured fork. Sprinkle tops with sugar. Bake until very light brown, 6 to 8 minutes.   2 dozen cookies.

Raisin Filling

1¾ cups raisins	2 tablespoons Gold Medal
¾ cup water	all-purpose flour
½ cup sugar	1 tablespoon lemon juice

Heat raisins and water to boiling; reduce heat. Cover and simmer 5 minutes. Mix sugar and flour; stir into raisin mixture. Heat to boiling over medium heat, stirring constantly. Boil and stir 1 minute. Stir in lemon juice; cool.

Cherry-Apricot Filling

½ cup sugar	¼ cup maraschino cherry
1 tablespoon plus 1	juice
teaspoon cornstarch	⅓ cup chopped maraschino
½ cup water	cherries
	⅓ cup cut-up dried apricots

Mix sugar and cornstarch in saucepan. Stir in remaining ingredients. Heat to rolling boil. Boil and stir 1 minute; cool.

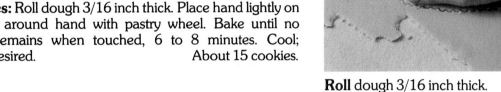

Roll dough 3/16 inch thick. Trace around hand with pastry wheel.

Spread uncut rounds with about 1 tablespoon of the filling. Top with cut rounds; press edges. Sprinkle tops with sugar.

Top to bottom: Hand Cookies, Sugar Cookies, Filled Sugar Cookies   47

CREAM WAFERS

2 cups Gold Medal
   all-purpose flour*
1 cup butter, softened

⅓ cup whipping cream
  Sugar
  Creamy Filling (below)

Mix flour, butter and whipping cream. Cover and refrigerate at least 1 hour.

Heat oven to 375°. Roll about ⅓ of the dough at a time ⅛ inch thick on floured cloth-covered board (keep remaining dough refrigerated until ready to roll). Cut into 1½-inch rounds.

Transfer rounds with metal spatula to piece of waxed paper that is heavily covered with sugar; turn to coat each round. Place about 1 inch apart on ungreased cookie sheet. Prick each round with fork about 4 times. Bake just until set but not brown, 7 to 9 minutes. Cool. Just before serving put cookies together in pairs with Creamy Filling.   About 5 dozen cookies.

*Self-rising flour can be used in this recipe.

Creamy Filling

Beat ¼ cup margarine or butter, softened, ¾ cup powdered sugar and 1 teaspoon vanilla until smooth and fluffy. Tint with few drops food color. Beat in few drops water, if necessary, until of spreading consistency.

Coat each round with sugar. Place on ungreased cookie sheet. Prick each round with fork several times.

Tint Creamy Filling with 1 or 2 drops food color if desired. Just before serving, spread about 1 teaspoon of the tinted filling between 2 cookies.

Great advances have been made over the years in the way recipes are written. An 1894 Washburn Crosby cookbook, for example, included a rolled cookie recipe similar to Cream Wafers, instructing the cook to "roll the dough as thin as pasteboard ... and bake in a quick oven."

OLD-FASHIONED MOLASSES COOKIES

1½	cups sugar	1½	teaspoons ground cinnamon
1	cup shortening		
2	eggs	1	teaspoon ground ginger
½	cup light or dark molasses	1	teaspoon ground cloves
3	teaspoons baking soda	1	teaspoon salt
½	cup water		Frosting (below)
5½	cups Gold Medal all-purpose flour		

Mix sugar, shortening, eggs and molasses. Dissolve baking soda in water; stir into molasses mixture. Stir in remaining ingredients except Frosting. Cover and refrigerate at least 2 hours.

Heat oven to 375°. Roll dough ¼ inch thick on lightly floured cloth-covered board. Cut with floured 2¾-inch round cookie cutter or other favorite cutter. Place about 2 inches apart on lightly greased cookie sheet. Bake until light brown, 8 to 10 minutes. Cool; generously frost bottoms of cookies with Frosting. Let stand 2 to 3 hours before storing to allow frosting to dry.

About 6 dozen cookies.

Frosting

1	envelope plus 2 teaspoons unflavored gelatin	2¼	cups powdered sugar
		1	teaspoon baking powder
1	cup cold water	1½	teaspoons vanilla
1	cup granulated sugar	⅛	teaspoon salt

Sprinkle gelatin on cold water in 2-quart saucepan to soften; stir in granulated sugar. Heat to rolling boil; reduce heat. Simmer uncovered 10 minutes. Pour hot mixture over powdered sugar in large mixer bowl; beat until foamy, about 2 minutes. Beat in remaining ingredients on high speed until stiff peaks form, 12 to 15 minutes.

Frost bottoms of cookies; decorate with colored sugar if desired. Let stand 2 to 3 hours before storing to allow frosting to dry.

Refrigerator cookies, also known as icebox or overnight cookies, grew popular during World War II when many women took jobs outside the home. With limited cooking time, Gold Medal users could prepare the dough ahead, refrigerate it and bake fresh cookies many times from one batch.

FRUIT-SLICE COOKIES

1 cup granulated sugar	1½ teaspoons grated lemon
1 cup margarine or butter,	peel
softened	1½ teaspoons grated lime
2 eggs	peel
1½ teaspoons vanilla	1½ teaspoons grated orange
3 cups Gold Medal	peel
all-purpose flour*	Yellow, green and orange
1 teaspoon salt	sugars
Yellow, green and red	
food colors	

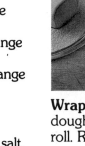

Mix sugar, margarine, eggs and vanilla. Stir in flour and salt. Divide dough into 4 equal parts. Mix few drops yellow food color and the lemon peel into 1 part. Mix few drops green food color and the lime peel into another part. Mix few drops each red and yellow food color and the orange peel into another part. Leave remaining part plain. (If necessary, work in food color and peel with hands.) Cover and refrigerate 1 hour.

Wrap 1 rectangle of plain dough around each colored roll. Roll in colored sugar.

Shape each part colored dough into roll, about 2 inches in diameter. Divide plain dough into 3 equal parts; roll each part into rectangle, 6×4 inches. Wrap rectangle around each roll of colored dough; press together. Roll in matching colored sugar. Wrap and refrigerate at least 4 hours.

Heat oven to 400°. Cut rolls into ⅛-inch slices; cut each slice into halves. Place about 1 inch apart on ungreased cookie sheet. Bake 6 to 8 minutes. Immediately remove from cookie sheet.

About 10 dozen cookies.

*Do not use self-rising flour in this recipe.

Cut rolls into ⅛ inch slices; cut each slice into halves. Bake, then decorate if desired.

DATE PINWHEELS

¾ pound pitted dates,	¼ cup margarine or butter,
cut up	softened
⅓ cup granulated sugar	1 egg
⅓ cup water	½ teaspoon vanilla
1 cup packed brown sugar	1¾ cups Gold Medal
¼ cup shortening	all-purpose flour*
	¼ teaspoon salt

Cook dates, granulated sugar and water, stirring constantly, until thickened; cool. Mix brown sugar, shortening, margarine, egg and vanilla until smooth. Stir in flour and salt. Divide dough into halves. Roll each half into rectangle, 11×7 inches, on waxed paper. Spread half of the date filling on each rectangle. Roll up tightly, beginning at 11-inch side. Pinch edge of dough into roll to seal. Wrap and refrigerate at least 4 hours.

Roll each half of dough into rectangle on waxed paper. Spread half of the date filling on each rectangle. Roll up rectangles tightly.

Heat oven to 400°. Cut rolls into ¼-inch slices. Place about 1 inch apart on ungreased cookie sheet. Bake until light brown, about 10 minutes. Immediately remove from cookie sheet.

About 5 dozen cookies.

*If using self-rising flour, omit salt.

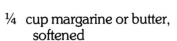

Main Dishes

SAVORY STEW WITH DUMPLINGS *(pictured on pages 52-53)*

½ cup Gold Medal
    all-purpose flour
2 to 3 teaspoons salt
¼ teaspoon pepper
2 pounds beef stew meat,
    cut into 1-inch pieces
3 tablespoons vegetable oil
4 cups water
1 bay leaf

2 tablespoons snipped
    parsley
½ teaspoon dried thyme
    leaves
1½ cups ¼-inch slices carrots
1 cup ¼-inch slices celery
2 medium onions, sliced
4 cups ¾-inch cubes
    unpared potatoes
    Herb Dumplings (below)

Mix flour, salt and pepper. Coat beef with flour mixture. Heat oil in Dutch oven until hot; add beef and remaining flour mixture. Cook and stir until beef is brown. Add water. Heat to boiling; reduce heat. Cover and simmer 1½ hours. Add bay leaf, parsley, thyme and vegetables. Cover and simmer 30 minutes.

Prepare Herb Dumplings. Drop by spoonfuls onto hot beef or vegetables (do not drop directly into liquid). Cook uncovered over low heat 10 minutes. Cover and cook 10 minutes longer.

6 to 8 servings.

Herb Dumplings

3 tablespoons shortening
1½ cups Gold Medal
    all-purpose flour*
2 teaspoons baking
    powder
¾ teaspoon salt

¼ teaspoon dried sage
    leaves
¼ teaspoon dried thyme
    leaves
¾ cup milk

Cut shortening into flour, baking powder, salt, sage and thyme until mixture resembles fine crumbs. Stir in milk.

*If using self-rising flour, omit baking powder and salt.

CORN FRITTERS

Vegetable oil
1 cup Gold Medal
    all-purpose flour*
1 teaspoon baking powder
1 teaspoon salt

2 eggs
½ cup milk
1 teaspoon vegetable oil
1 can (16 ounces) whole
    kernel corn, drained

Heat oil (3 to 4 inches) in deep-fat fryer or electric skillet to 375°. Mix remaining ingredients except corn with hand beater until smooth. Stir in corn. Drop by rounded tablespoonfuls into hot oil. Fry until deep golden brown, about 5 minutes; drain on paper towels. Serve with maple-flavored syrup if desired.

6 to 8 servings.

*If using self-rising flour, omit baking powder and salt.

Ham Fritters: Omit salt and corn. Stir in 1 cup cut-up fully cooked smoked ham.

CLASSIC CHICKEN CURRY CREPES

Crepes (below)
1 pound asparagus
¼ cup margarine or butter
¾ cup finely chopped onion
¼ cup Gold Medal
   all-purpose flour
1 tablespoon plus 2
   teaspoons curry powder
¾ teaspoon salt

2 cups milk
2 cups half-and-half
2½ cups cubed cooked
   chicken
1 cup golden raisins
2 tablespoons flaked or
   shredded coconut
1 cup sliced almonds

Prepare Crepes. Break off tough ends of asparagus as far down as stalks snap easily, making each spear the length of a crepe. Wash asparagus thoroughly. Remove scales if sandy or tough. Tie whole stalks in a bundle with string. Heat 1 inch salted water (½ teaspoon salt to 1 cup water) to boiling in deep narrow pan or coffeepot. Place asparagus upright in pan. Heat to boiling; cook uncovered 5 minutes. Cover and cook until stalks are crisp-tender, 5 minutes longer. Drain; cut each spear crosswise into halves.

Heat margarine in 10-inch skillet over low heat until melted. Cook and stir onion in margarine until tender. Stir in flour, curry powder and salt. Cook over low heat, stirring constantly, until bubbly. Remove from heat; gradually stir in milk and half-and-half. Heat to boiling, stirring constantly. Boil and stir 1 minute. Remove from heat; reserve 2 cups sauce for top of crepes. Stir chicken, raisins and coconut into remaining sauce.

Place 2 asparagus spear halves one-third the distance from edge of each crepe; top with about ¼ cup chicken mixture. Roll up; place in 2 ungreased baking dishes, 11×7×1½ inches, or oven-proof serving platter. Cover with heavy-duty aluminum foil.

Heat oven to 350°. Bake until hot, about 25 minutes. Heat reserved sauce. Top crepes with sauce and sprinkle with almonds. Serve immediately.   6 servings.

Crepes

1½ cups Gold Medal
   all-purpose flour
1 tablespoon sugar
½ teaspoon baking powder
½ teaspoon salt

2 cups milk
2 eggs
½ teaspoon vanilla
2 tablespoons margarine or
   butter, melted

Mix flour, sugar, baking powder and salt. Stir in remaining ingredients. Beat with hand beater until smooth.

Lightly butter 6-, 7- or 8-inch skillet; heat over medium heat until bubbly. For each crepe, pour scant ¼ cup of batter into skillet; immediately rotate skillet until thin film of batter covers bottom. Cook until light brown. Run wide spatula around edge to loosen; turn and cook other side until light brown. Stack crepes, placing waxed paper or paper towel between each. Keep crepes covered to prevent them from drying out.

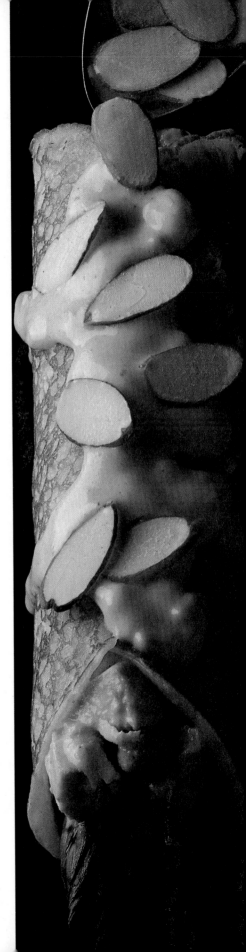

PARSLEY PINWHEELS AND HAM BAKE

2 cups cut-up fully cooked smoked ham	½ teaspoon dry mustard
1 can (10¾ ounces) condensed cream of chicken soup	⅓ cup shortening
	1¾ cups Gold Medal all-purpose flour*
½ cup chopped green pepper	2½ teaspoons baking powder
½ cup chopped onion	¾ teaspoon salt
1 jar (2 ounces) chopped pimiento, drained	¾ cup milk
	½ cup snipped parsley

Heat oven to 425°. Mix ham, soup, green pepper, onion, pimiento and mustard; pour into ungreased baking dish, 8×8×2 inches.

Cut shortening into flour, baking powder and salt with pastry blender until mixture resembles fine crumbs. Stir in just enough milk so dough leaves side of bowl and rounds up into a ball. Turn dough onto lightly floured surface. Knead lightly 10 times. Roll into rectangle, 12×9 inches; sprinkle with parsley. Roll up, beginning at narrow end; pinch edge to seal. Cut into 1-inch slices. Arrange slices, cut sides up, on ham mixture. Bake until biscuits are golden brown, 20 to 30 minutes. 6 to 8 servings.

*If using self-rising flour, omit baking powder and salt.

CORNISH BEEF PASTIES

Pastry (below)
2 cups diced pared potatoes
1 pound beef chuck or top round steak, cut into ½-inch pieces
2 cups diced carrots
1 cup chopped onion
1 cup sliced mushrooms
Seasoning (below)
4 tablespoons margarine or butter
4 tablespoons water
Milk
Wine Sauce (below)

Heat oven to 350°. Prepare pastry; divide into 4 equal parts. Roll each part into 12-inch circle on lightly floured cloth-covered board. Place pastry circle on end of ungreased large cookie sheet. Layer ¼ each of the potatoes, beef, carrots, onion and mushrooms on half of the pastry circle. Sprinkle with about ½ teaspoon Seasoning; dot with 1 tablespoon margarine. Sprinkle 1 tablespoon water over filling. Brush edge of pastry with water. Fold pastry over filling. Turn edge of lower pastry over edge of top pastry; seal. Flute if desired. Prick top with fork; brush with milk. Repeat with remaining pastry circles (use 1 cookie sheet for 2 pasties). Bake until golden brown, 55 to 60 minutes. Serve with Wine Sauce.   4 pasties.

Layer potatoes, beef, carrots, onion and mushrooms on half of each pastry circle. Sprinkle with Seasoning.

Pastry

1½ cups shortening
4 cups Gold Medal all-purpose flour
2 teaspoons salt
½ cup water

Cut shortening into flour and salt until particles are size of small peas. Sprinkle in water, 1 tablespoon at a time, tossing with fork until all flour is moistened and pastry almost cleans side of bowl. Gather pastry into a ball.

Seasoning

Mix 1 teaspoon salt, ½ teaspoon dried dill weed, ½ teaspoon dried basil leaves and ¼ teaspoon pepper.

Wine Sauce

¼ cup margarine or butter
¼ cup Gold Medal all-purpose flour
1½ cups beef broth (bouillon)
½ cup red wine
½ teaspoon snipped parsley

Heat margarine over low heat until golden brown. Stir in flour. Cook over low heat, stirring constantly, until deep brown. Remove from heat; stir in broth and wine. Heat to boiling, stirring constantly. Boil and stir 1 minute. Stir in parsley.

Betty Crocker

Betty Crocker

To create the signature of Betty Crocker, a contest was conducted among all women employees of the Washburn Crosby Company in 1921. The most distinctive and appropriate handwriting was chosen. That signature has remained basically the same over the years.

HAM SHORTCAKES

Baking Powder Biscuits
(page 26)
1 can (4½ ounces) deviled
ham
½ cup shredded Cheddar
cheese (about 2 ounces)

2 tablespoons mayonnaise
or salad dressing
1 teaspoon instant minced
onion
Milk
Tomato Sauce (below)

Heat oven to 450°. Prepare Baking Powder Biscuits as directed
except — after kneading, roll into rectangle, 14×10 inches. Cut
with floured 2¾-inch doughnut cutter that has center removed.
Place half of the circles in greased baking dish, 8×8×2 inches.
Mix ham, cheese, mayonnaise and onion; spread about 1
tablespoon on each biscuit in dish. Top with remaining biscuits.
Brush tops with milk. Bake until golden brown, 15 to 20 minutes.
Serve with Tomato Sauce.   9 shortcakes.

Tomato Sauce

1 can (16 ounces) tomato
sauce
1 green onion, sliced

¼ teaspoon dry mustard
¼ teaspoon sugar

Mix all ingredients in 1-quart saucepan. Heat to boiling over
medium heat; reduce heat. Simmer uncovered 10 minutes.

*This 1931 advertisement which
promoted Ham Shortcakes,
three-time winner at the Vernon
County Fair in Louisiana,
informed the reader that the recipe
was available free in the bag of
Gold Medal flour. Packing recipes
in flour bags became a long-
standing Gold Medal tradition
which began in 1928 to celebrate
the formation of General Mills, Inc.*

CREAM SAUCE SUPPERS

Cream Sauce

¼ cup margarine or butter
¼ cup Gold Medal
    all-purpose flour
¼ teaspoon salt
¼ teaspoon pepper
2 cups half-and-half

Heat margarine in 2-quart saucepan over low heat until melted. Mix in flour, salt and pepper. Cook over low heat, stirring constantly, until smooth and bubbly; remove from heat. Stir in half-and-half. Heat to boiling over medium heat, stirring constantly. Boil and stir 1 minute; remove from heat. Use sauce in one of the following recipes.

Macaroni and Cheese

8 ounces uncooked elbow
    macaroni (about 2 cups)
    Cream Sauce (above)
8 ounces process American
    cheese loaf, cut into cubes

Heat oven to 375°. Butter 1½-quart round casserole. Cook macaroni as directed on package; drain. Prepare Cream Sauce. Stir in cheese. Heat over medium heat, stirring constantly, until cheese is melted.

Layer ⅓ each of the macaroni and cheese sauce in casserole; repeat 2 times. Bake uncovered until golden brown, about 35 minutes. Garnish with parsley or green pepper rings if desired.

                                    4 to 6 servings.

Macaroni and Cheese

Creamed Chicken and Biscuits

    Baking Powder Biscuits
    (page 26)
    Cream Sauce (above)
½ cup chicken broth
1 can (4 ounces) mushroom
    stems and pieces, drained
½ cup chopped green
    pepper
1 jar (2 ounces) sliced
    pimiento, drained
3 cups cubed cooked
    chicken or turkey

Prepare Baking Powder Biscuits. Prepare Cream Sauce as directed except—stir in chicken broth with the half-and-half. Heat to boiling over medium heat, stirring constantly. Boil and stir 1 minute; reduce heat. Stir in mushrooms, green pepper, pimiento and chicken; heat through.

Split each biscuit into halves; spoon creamed chicken over top. Garnish with parsley if desired.   4 to 6 servings.

*Creamed Chicken
and Biscuits*

SOUTH-OF-THE-BORDER PIE

Cornmeal Pastry (below)
1 can (16 ounces) refried
   beans
1 can (4 ounces) green
   chilies, drained and
   chopped
2 to 4 drops red pepper
   sauce
1 avocado

¼ cup dairy sour cream
1 tablespoon lemon juice
2 tomatoes, chopped
½ cup chopped onion
¼ cup shredded Cheddar
   cheese
¼ cup chopped green
   pepper

Heat oven to 475°. Prepare Cornmeal Pastry. Bake until light brown, 8 to 10 minutes; cool.

Reduce oven temperature to 400°. Mix beans, chilies and pepper sauce; spread over crust. Mash avocado. Mix in sour cream and lemon juice; reserve. Arrange tomatoes in ring around edge of pan. Arrange onion in ring next to tomatoes. Spoon reserved avocado mixture into ring next to onion; sprinkle avocado mixture with cheese. Place green pepper in center. Bake until hot and cheese is melted, about 15 minutes.   4 servings or 16 appetizers.

Cornmeal Pastry

⅓ cup plus 1 tablespoon
   shortening or ⅓ cup lard
1 cup Gold Medal
   all-purpose flour*

¼ cup yellow cornmeal
½ teaspoon salt
3 to 4 tablespoons cold
   water

Cut shortening into flour, cornmeal and salt until particles are size of small peas. Sprinkle in water, 1 tablespoon at a time, tossing with fork until all flour is moistened and pastry almost cleans side of bowl. Gather pastry into a ball; shape into flattened round on lightly floured cloth-covered board. Roll pastry 1 inch larger than inverted 12-inch pizza pan. Fold pastry into quarters; place in pan. Unfold and ease into pan, pressing firmly against bottom and side. Trim overhanging edge of pastry 1 inch from rim of pan. Fold and roll pastry under, even with pan; flute if desired. Prick bottom and side thoroughly with fork.

*If using self-rising flour, omit salt.

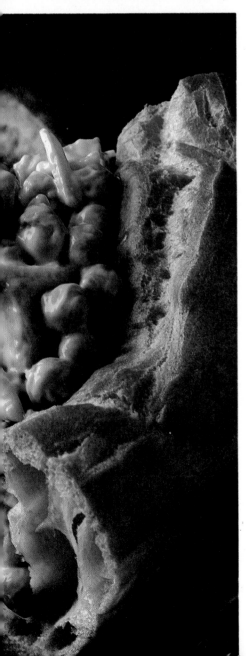

SALAD BOWL PUFF

½ cup water
¼ cup margarine or butter
½ cup Gold Medal
    all-purpose flour*
⅛ teaspoon salt

2 eggs
Ham Salad Filling or
    Tuna Salad Filling
    (below)

Heat oven to 400°. Grease pie plate, 9×1¼ inches. Heat water and margarine to rolling boil. Stir in flour and salt. Stir vigorously over low heat until mixture forms a ball, about 30 seconds. Remove from heat; cool 10 minutes. Beat in eggs, all at once; continue beating until smooth. Spread dough evenly in pie plate, building up edge slightly. Bake until puffed and dry in center, 45 to 60 minutes; cool. Just before serving, fill with Ham Salad Filling. Cut into wedges.   6 servings.

*Do not use self-rising flour in this recipe.

Ham Salad Filling

1 package (10 ounces)
    frozen green peas
2 cups cubed fully cooked
    smoked ham
1 cup shredded Cheddar
    cheese (about 4 ounces)

2 tablespoons chopped
    onion
¾ cup mayonnaise or salad
    dressing
1½ teaspoons prepared
    mustard

Rinse frozen peas under running cold water to separate; drain. Mix all ingredients. Cover and refrigerate at least 2 hours.

Tuna Salad Filling

2 cans (6½ ounces each)
    tuna, drained, or 2 cups
    cut-up cooked chicken
1 cup chopped celery
½ cup chopped green olives
¼ cup chopped onion

¾ to 1 cup mayonnaise or
    salad dressing
3 hard-cooked eggs,
    chopped
1 teaspoon lemon juice

Mix all ingredients. Cover and refrigerate at least 2 hours.

SUPPER POPOVER

1 pound ground beef
1 can (15 ounces) tomato
  sauce
¼ cup chopped green
  pepper
2 tablespoons Gold Medal
  all-purpose flour*
½ teaspoon salt
½ teaspoon pepper
1 teaspoon parsley flakes

2 cups shredded Cheddar
  cheese (about 8 ounces)
2 eggs
1 cup milk
1 tablespoon vegetable oil
1 cup Gold Medal
  all-purpose flour*
½ teaspoon salt
2 tablespoons chopped
  green onions

Heat oven to 425°. Cook and stir ground beef in 10-inch skillet until brown; drain. Stir in tomato sauce, green pepper, 2 tablespoons flour, ½ teaspoon salt, the pepper and parsley flakes. Heat to boiling. Boil and stir 1 minute. Pour into ungreased baking pan, 13×9×2 inches. Sprinkle cheese on top.

Beat eggs, milk, oil, 1 cup flour and ½ teaspoon salt with hand beater; pour over cheese. Sprinkle with onions. Bake until puffy and golden brown, 25 to 30 minutes. Serve immediately.

6 servings.

*Do not use self-rising flour in this recipe.

THREE BEAN AND CORN BREAD CASSEROLE

2 cans (21 ounces each)
  baked beans
2 cans (15 ounces each)
  kidney beans, drained
1 can (8½ ounces) lima
  beans, drained
1 can (8 ounces) tomato
  sauce
¼ cup catsup

2 tablespoons packed brown
  sugar
2 tablespoons instant
  minced onion
½ teaspoon dry mustard
½ teaspoon salt
¼ teaspoon pepper
  Corn Bread Topping
  (below)

Heat oven to 425°. Mix all ingredients except Corn Bread Topping; pour into ungreased baking dish, 13×9×2 inches. Prepare Corn Bread Topping; spoon evenly over bean mixture to within 1 inch of edges. Bake until topping is deep golden brown, 25 to 30 minutes. 8 servings.

Corn Bread Topping

⅔ cup Gold Medal
  all-purpose flour*
⅓ cup yellow cornmeal
1 tablespoon sugar
1 teaspoon baking powder

½ teaspoon salt
1 egg
½ cup milk
2 tablespoons margarine or
  butter, softened

Beat all ingredients with hand beater until smooth.

*If using self-rising flour, omit baking powder and salt.

HAMBURGER CREOLE PIE

Pastry (below)
1 pound ground beef
1 can (16 ounces) whole
   tomatoes
1 can (12 ounces) whole
   kernel corn
½ cup chopped green
   pepper
½ cup chopped onion
¼ cup Gold Medal
   all-purpose flour
½ teaspoon chili powder
½ teaspoon salt
½ teaspoon pepper
3 green pepper rings

Heat oven to 400°. Prepare pastry. Cook and stir ground beef in 10-inch skillet until brown; drain. Drain tomatoes, reserving ¼ cup liquid. Stir tomatoes, reserved tomato liquid, corn (with liquid) and the remaining ingredients except green pepper rings into beef. Heat to boiling; reduce heat. Simmer uncovered, stirring constantly, until thickened, about 1 minute.

Spoon beef mixture into pastry-lined pie plate. Bake until crust is golden brown, 25 to 30 minutes. Garnish with green pepper rings.

6 servings

Pastry

3 tablespoons shortening
1½ cups Gold Medal
   all-purpose flour*
1½ teaspoons baking
   powder
½ teaspoon salt
1 egg
⅓ cup milk

Cut shortening into flour, baking powder and salt with pastry blender until mixture resembles fine crumbs. Stir in egg and milk. Gather pastry into a ball. Roll 2 inches larger than inverted pie plate, 9×1¼ inches, on lightly floured cloth-covered board. Fold pastry into quarters; place in plate. Unfold and ease into plate; flute if desired.

*If using self-rising flour, omit salt in beef mixture and baking powder and salt in pastry.

Beginning in 1942, flour was enriched in accordance with government regulations. Gold Medal advertisements explained the vitamin and mineral additions and offered consumers a booklet, Thru Highway to Good Nutrition, which earned national recognition from the American Red Cross. Many of these advertisements also emphasized the importance of "nutritious, no-waste eating" in wartime.

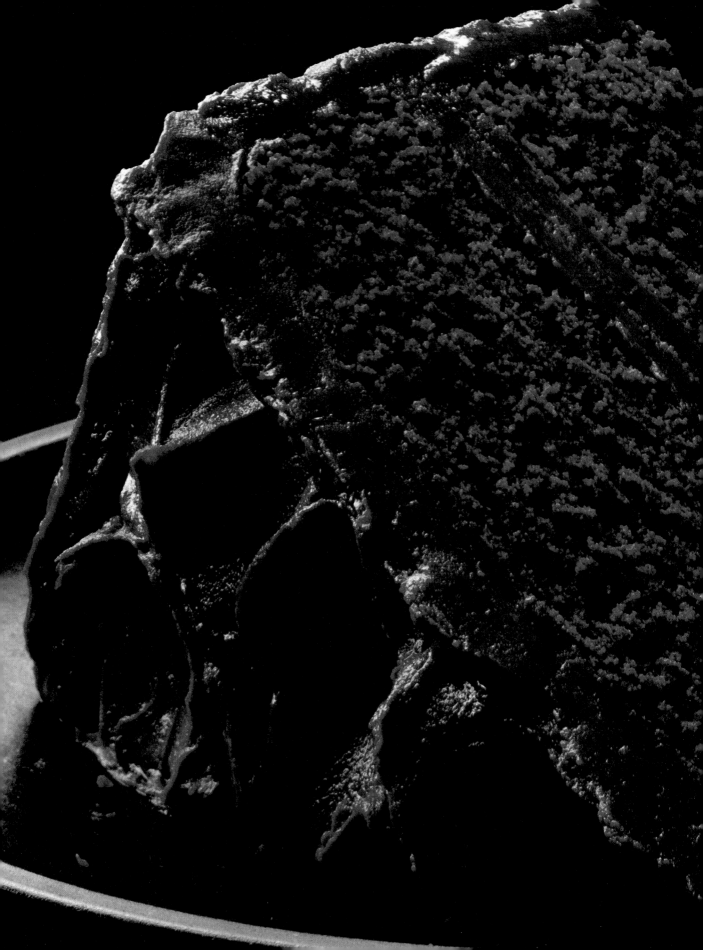

Desserts

APPLE CRISP

4 cups sliced pared baking apples (about 4 medium)	½ cup regular oats
⅔ to ¾ cup packed brown sugar	¾ teaspoon ground cinnamon
½ cup Gold Medal all-purpose flour*	¾ teaspoon ground nutmeg
	⅓ cup margarine or butter, softened

Heat oven to 375°. Grease baking pan, 8×8×2 inches. Arrange apples in pan. Mix remaining ingredients with fork; sprinkle over apples. Bake until apples are tender and topping is golden brown, about 30 minutes. Serve with cream, ice cream or hard sauce if desired.   6 servings.

*Self-rising flour can be used in this recipe.

Cherry Crisp: Substitute 1 can (21 ounces) cherry pie filling for the apples and use lesser amount of sugar.

Peach Crisp: Substitute 1 can (29 ounces) sliced peaches, drained, for the apples and use lesser amount of sugar.

FRESH FRUIT COBBLER

1 cup sugar
3 tablespoons cornstarch
¾ teaspoon ground
    cinnamon
3 cups sliced peeled
    peaches or nectarines
    (5 to 6 medium)
2 cups sliced unpeeled
    red plums (6 to 8 large)
1 cup blueberries

1 cup Gold Medal
    all-purpose flour*
2 tablespoons sugar
1½ teaspoons baking
    powder
½ teaspoon salt
⅓ cup shortening
3 tablespoons milk
1 egg

Heat oven to 375°. Mix 1 cup sugar, the cornstarch and cinnamon in 3-quart saucepan. Stir in peaches and plums. Cook, stirring constantly, until mixture thickens and boils. Boil and stir 1 minute. Stir in blueberries. Pour into ungreased baking dish, 8×8×2 inches.

Mix flour, 2 tablespoons sugar, the baking powder and salt. Cut in shortening. Mix in milk and egg. Drop dough by 9 spoonfuls onto hot fruit mixture. Bake until topping is golden brown, 25 to 30 minutes. Serve with cream or ice cream if desired.   9 servings.

*If using self-rising flour, omit baking powder and salt.

Note: Other combinations of fresh fruit totaling 6 cups can be substituted (purple plums, berries, cut-up rhubarb, cherries).

RHUBARB-MERINGUE DESSERT

½ cup margarine or
    butter, softened
1 cup Gold Medal
    all-purpose flour*
1 tablespoon sugar
3 eggs, separated
1 cup sugar

2 tablespoons Gold Medal
    all-purpose flour
¼ teaspoon salt
½ cup half-and-half
2½ cups cut-up rhubarb
⅓ cup sugar
1 teaspoon vanilla
¼ cup flaked coconut

Heat oven to 350°. Mix margarine, 1 cup flour and 1 tablespoon sugar. Press in ungreased baking pan, 9×9×2 inches. Bake 10 minutes. Mix egg yolks, 1 cup sugar, 2 tablespoons flour, the salt and half-and-half; stir in rhubarb. Pour over baked layer. Bake 45 minutes.

Beat egg whites until foamy. Beat in ⅓ cup sugar, 1 tablespoon at a time; continue beating until stiff and glossy. Do not underbeat. Beat in vanilla. Spread over rhubarb mixture; sprinkle with coconut. Bake until light brown, about 10 minutes.   9 servings.

*Self-rising flour can be used in this recipe.

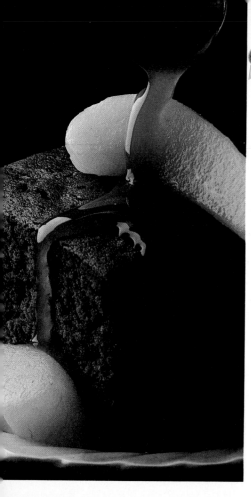

⊕ GINGERBREAD WITH BUTTERSCOTCH-PEAR SAUCE

2⅓ cups Gold Medal all-purpose flour*	1 teaspoon baking soda
⅓ cup sugar	1 teaspoon ground ginger
1 cup light or dark molasses	1 teaspoon ground cinnamon
¾ cup hot water	¾ teaspoon salt
½ cup shortening	Butterscotch-Pear Sauce (below)
1 egg	

Heat oven to 325°. Grease and flour baking pan, 9×9×2 inches. Beat all ingredients except sauce in large mixer bowl on low speed, scraping bowl constantly, 30 seconds. Beat on medium speed, scraping bowl occasionally, 3 minutes. Pour into pan. Bake until wooden pick inserted in center comes out clean, about 50 minutes. Top with Butterscotch-Pear Sauce.   9 servings.

*Do not use self-rising flour in this recipe.

Butterscotch-Pear Sauce

1 cup packed brown sugar	2 teaspoons grated lemon peel
½ cup light corn syrup	1 can (16 ounces) sliced pears, drained
¼ cup margarine or butter	
½ cup half-and-half	

Mix brown sugar, corn syrup, margarine and half-and-half in 1½-quart saucepan. Cook over low heat, stirring occasionally, 5 minutes. Stir in lemon peel and pears; heat through.

HOT FUDGE PUDDING CAKE

1 cup Gold Medal all-purpose flour*	2 tablespoons vegetable oil
¾ cup granulated sugar	1 teaspoon vanilla
2 tablespoons cocoa	1 cup chopped nuts, if desired
2 teaspoons baking powder	1 cup packed brown sugar
¼ teaspoon salt	¼ cup cocoa
½ cup milk	1¾ cups hottest tap water
	Ice cream

Heat oven to 350°. Mix flour, granulated sugar, 2 tablespoons cocoa, the baking powder and salt in ungreased baking pan, 9×9×2 inches. Mix in milk, oil and vanilla with fork until smooth. Stir in nuts. Spread in pan. Sprinkle with brown sugar and ¼ cup cocoa. Pour hot water over batter. Bake 40 minutes. Let stand 15 minutes; spoon into dessert dishes or cut into squares and invert on dessert plates. Top with ice cream and spoon sauce over each serving.   9 servings.

*If using self-rising flour, omit baking powder and salt.

Hot Fudge-Butterscotch Pudding Cake: Substitute 1 package (6 ounces) butterscotch chips for the nuts. Decrease brown sugar to ½ cup and the ¼ cup cocoa to 2 tablespoons.

The recipe for Apple Dumplings was available free in the Gold Medal flour bag, as noted in this 1938 advertisement. It was highlighted again in Gold Medal advertisements of 1940 and 1947. This recipe also has been included in many of the company's cookbooks over the years, beginning with the 1904 Christmas Edition Gold Medal Flour Cook Book.

APPLE DUMPLINGS

Pastry for 9-inch
Two-Crust Pie
(page 85)
6 baking apples (each
about 3 inches in
diameter), pared
and cored

3 tablespoons raisins
3 tablespoons chopped
nuts
2½ cups packed brown
sugar
1⅓ cups water

Heat oven to 425°. Prepare pastry. Gather into a ball. Roll ⅔ of the pastry into ´14-inch square on lightly floured cloth-covered board with floured stockinet-covered rolling pin; cut into 4 squares. Roll remaining pastry into rectangle, 14×7 inches; cut into 2 squares. Place apple on each square.

Mix raisins and nuts; fill each apple. Moisten corners of each pastry square; bring 2 opposite corners up over apple and pinch. Repeat with remaining corners; pinch edges of pastry to seal. Place dumplings in ungreased baking dish, 13×9×2 inches.

Heat brown sugar and water to boiling; carefully pour around dumplings. Bake, spooning or basting syrup over dumplings 2 or 3 times, until crust is golden and apples are tender, about 40 minutes. Serve warm or cool with cream or sweetened whipped cream if desired.   6 dumplings.

Moisten corners of pastry square; bring opposite corners together and pinch. Repeat with other corners. Pinch edges of pastry together.

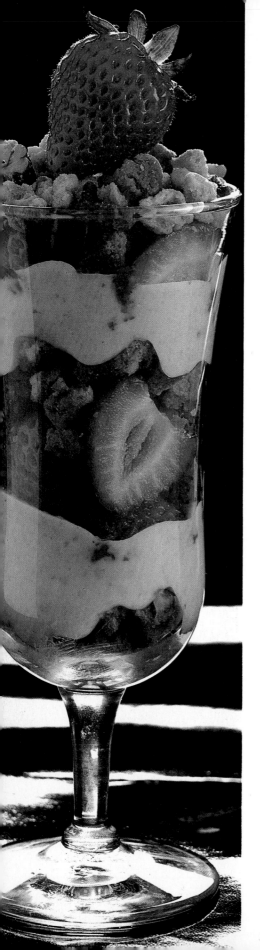

BUTTER CRUNCH DESSERTS

Berry Parfaits: For each serving, alternate layers of 1 tablespoon Butter Crunch (below), 2 tablespoons fruit-flavored yogurt and 2 tablespoons fresh berries; repeat. Top with 1 tablespoon Butter Crunch. Garnish with berries. (Suggested combinations: lemon-flavored yogurt and blueberries, strawberry-flavored yogurt and strawberry halves, raspberry-flavored yogurt and raspberries.)

Cinnamon-Applesauce Dessert: Mix 2 cups applesauce and 1 teaspoon cinnamon. Top with 1 cup sweetened whipped cream and sprinkle with 1 cup Butter Crunch (below).   6 servings.

Fruit-Custard Dessert: For each serving, pour chilled soft custard over fresh berries or fruit (oranges, bananas, peaches, strawberries). Sprinkle with Butter Crunch (below).

Pudding Dessert: Prepare your favorite flavor pudding and pie filling as directed on package for pudding except—pour into shallow serving dish. After refrigerating, sprinkle with 1 cup Butter Crunch (below). Serve with cream.   6 servings.

Butter Crunch

½ cup butter
¼ cup packed brown sugar
1 cup Gold Medal
   all-purpose flour*

½ cup chopped pecans,
   chopped walnuts or
   flaked coconut

Heat oven to 400°. Mix all ingredients with hands. Spread in ungreased baking pan, 13×9×2 inches. Bake 15 minutes; stir. Cool; cover and store in refrigerator.   2½ cups crunch.

*Do not use self-rising flour in this recipe.

During the 1950s, basic recipes with variations were popular advertising features. Butter Crunch was introduced with this 1956 advertisement as a versatile mixture which could become a pie crust, a cobbler ingredient or a topper for sundaes, pudding, fruit and custard.

70

PEACH-ALMOND SHORTCAKE

2 cups Gold Medal all-purpose flour	1 tablespoon margarine or butter, softened
2 tablespoons sugar	¼ cup packed brown sugar
3 teaspoons baking powder	½ cup slivered almonds
1 teaspoon salt	Almond Whipped Cream (below)
⅓ cup shortening	
¾ cup milk	4 cups sweetened sliced peeled peaches

Heat oven to 450°. Grease round pan, 9 × 1½ inches. Mix flour, 2 tablespoons sugar, the baking powder and salt. Cut in shortening. Stir in milk. Spread in pan; brush with margarine. Sprinkle with brown sugar and almonds. Bake until golden brown, about 20 minutes. Remove from pan; cool slightly. Split shortcake to make 2 layers. Fill layers with half of the Almond Whipped Cream and peaches. Top each serving with remaining whipped cream and peaches.   6 to 8 servings.

Almond Whipped Cream

Beat 1 cup chilled whipping cream, 3 tablespoons sugar and ½ teaspoon almond extract in chilled bowl until soft peaks form.

CREAM PUFFS

1 cup water	4 eggs
½ cup margarine or butter	Ice cream
1 cup Gold Medal all-purpose flour*	Chocolate Fudge Sauce (below)

Heat oven to 400°. Heat water and margarine to rolling boil in 1-quart saucepan. Stir in flour. Stir vigorously over low heat until mixture forms a ball, about 1 minute. Remove from heat; cool 10 minutes. Beat in eggs, all at once; continue beating until smooth. Drop dough by scant ¼ cupfuls about 3 inches apart onto ungreased cookie sheet. Bake until puffed and golden, 35 to 40 minutes. Cool away from draft. Cut off tops; pull out any filaments of soft dough. Fill puffs with ice cream; replace tops. Drizzle with Chocolate Fudge Sauce.   12 cream puffs.

*Self-rising flour can be used in this recipe.

Chocolate Fudge Sauce

1 package (12 ounces) semisweet chocolate chips or 4 bars (4 ounces each) sweet cooking chocolate	½ cup sugar
	½ cup water
	½ cup half-and-half or evaporated milk

Heat chocolate, sugar and water over low heat, stirring constantly, until chocolate and sugar are melted; remove from heat. Stir in half-and-half.

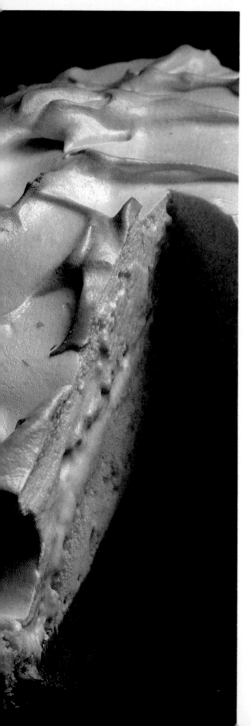

RASPBERRY-ALMOND CREPES

Crepes (page 55)
1 package (3¾ ounces)
   vanilla instant pudding
   and pie filling
2 cups half-and-half
½ teaspoon almond extract

2 tablespoons cornstarch
2 packages (10 ounces each)
   frozen raspberries,
   thawed
   Sliced almonds

Prepare Crepes. Prepare pudding and pie filling as directed on package for pudding except—substitute half-and-half for the milk and beat in almond extract; refrigerate until chilled.

Place cornstarch in 1½-quart saucepan; gradually stir in raspberries. Cook over medium heat, stirring constantly, until mixture thickens and boils. Boil and stir 1 minute; cool. Spoon generous 2 tablespoons of pudding mixture onto each crepe; roll up. Place 2 crepes, seam sides down, on each dessert plate. Top with raspberry mixture and sprinkle with almonds.

6 servings (2 crepes each).

BAKED ALASKA PUMPKIN PIE

Pastry for 9-inch
   One-Crust
   Pie (page 85)
3 egg yolks, slightly beaten
1 can (16 ounces) pumpkin
¾ cup sugar
1 teaspoon ground
   cinnamon
½ teaspoon salt

½ teaspoon ground ginger
¼ teaspoon ground cloves
1 can (13 ounces)
   evaporated milk
1 pint vanilla, toffee chip or
   butter pecan ice cream
   Brown Sugar Meringue
   (page 91)

Heat oven to 425°. Prepare pastry. Mix remaining ingredients except ice cream and meringue. Pour into pastry-lined pie plate. Bake 15 minutes. Reduce oven temperature to 350°; bake pie until knife inserted in center comes out clean, about 45 minutes longer. Refrigerate baked.pie at least 1 hour. Soften ice cream slightly; press into waxed paper-lined pie plate, 8×1½ inches. Freeze until solid.

Just before serving, heat oven to 500°. Prepare Brown Sugar Meringue. Unmold ice cream and invert on pie; remove waxed paper. Spoon meringue onto pie, covering ice cream completely and sealing meringue to edge of crust. Bake until golden brown, 2 to 3 minutes. Serve immediately.

BLACK FOREST CHERRY TORTE

Bonnie Butter Cake
(page 79)
Cherry Filling (below)
1½ cups chilled whipping
cream
¼ cup powdered sugar
⅓ bar (4-ounce size) sweet
cooking chocolate,
grated

Bake Bonnie Butter Cake in 9-inch layers as directed. Cool 10 minutes; remove from pans. Cool completely. Prepare Cherry Filling; refrigerate until chilled.

To assemble cake, place 1 layer, top side down, on serving plate. Beat whipping cream and powdered sugar in chilled bowl until very stiff. Form thin rim of whipped cream around edge of layer with decorators' tube or spoon. Fill center with Cherry Filling. Place other layer, top side up, on filling. Gently spread whipped cream on side and top of cake. Gently press chocolate by teaspoonfuls onto side of cake.

Place remaining whipped cream in decorators' tube with star tip. Pipe border of whipped cream around top edge of cake. Beginning from center of cake, outline individual portions in spoke design. Place desired number of reserved dipped cherries in each portion. Store torte in refrigerator.

Cherry Filling

2 tablespoons cornstarch
2 tablespoons sugar
1 can (16 ounces) pitted dark
sweet cherries
1 tablespoon brandy
flavoring

Mix cornstarch and sugar in 1-quart saucepan. Drain cherries, reserving syrup. Add enough water to reserved cherry syrup to measure 1 cup; stir into sugar-cornstarch mixture. Cook, stirring constantly, until mixture thickens and boils. Boil and stir 1 minute. Cool to lukewarm.

Stir in brandy flavoring. Dip 36 cherries into thickened syrup; reserve for top of cake. Cut remaining cherries into fourths and stir into thickened syrup.

The assurance of baking success with Gold Medal "Kitchen-tested" flour and recipes began in 1925. Washburn Crosby home economists tested recipes and flour, until perfect results were achieved. Then a cross-section of the nation's homemakers was selected to conduct tests in their own family kitchens. Home testing is conducted today by a 1900-member national consumer panel.

73

LEMON CHIFFON CAKE

2 cups Gold Medal all-purpose flour*	¾ cup cold water
1½ cups sugar	2 teaspoons grated lemon peel
3 teaspoons baking powder	2 teaspoons vanilla
1 teaspoon salt	1 cup egg whites (7 or 8)
½ cup vegetable oil	½ teaspoon cream of tartar
7 egg yolks	Lemon Butter Frosting (below)

Heat oven to 325°. Mix flour, sugar, baking powder and salt in bowl. Make a well and add in order: oil, egg yolks, water, lemon peel and vanilla. Beat with spoon until smooth. Beat egg whites and cream of tartar in large mixer bowl on high speed until stiff peaks form. Pour egg yolk mixture gradually over beaten whites, gently folding with rubber spatula just until blended. Pour into ungreased tube pan, 10×4 inches.

Bake until top springs back when touched lightly, about 1¼ hours. Invert pan on funnel; let hang until cake is cold. Remove from pan. Frost with Lemon Butter Frosting.

*If using self-rising flour, omit baking powder and salt.

Lemon Butter Frosting

Mix ⅓ cup margarine or butter, softened, and 3 cups powdered sugar. Beat in ½ teaspoon grated lemon peel and about 2 tablespoons lemon juice until of spreading consistency.

Orange Chiffon Cake: Substitute 2 tablespoons grated orange peel for the lemon peel and omit vanilla. Frost with Orange Butter Frosting (page 82).

Pour about ¼ of the egg yolk mixture at a time over beaten egg whites. Gently fold in by cutting rubber scraper down through the center of the whites, along the bottom and up the side, until mixtures are blended.

¶Introduced in 1948, Chiffon Cake was "the cake discovery of the century!" The cake was described as being light as angel food, rich as butter cake and easy to make. The mystery ingredient — new to cake-making — was salad or cooking oil.

Harry Baker, a 64-year-old California insurance salesman, invented Chiffon Cake in 1927. The unusual cake became known throughout the Los Angeles area, and upon request, Baker would prepare it for movie appearances and for famous Hollywood restaurants. The recipe, however, remained Baker's closely guarded secret for 20 years.

Over the years, Baker struck up a "friendship" with Betty Crocker while listening to her radio programs. Deciding that she should be the one to share the recipe with American homemakers, Baker traveled to Minneapolis and disclosed the baking secret to General Mills. Test kitchen home economists adapted it to typical home-baking techniques, created flavor variations on the original recipe and — with Baker's help — introduced to the American public the first really new type of cake in 100 years...Chiffon Cake.

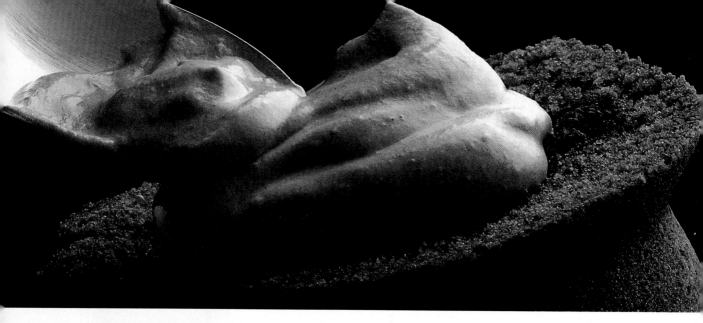

CHOCOLATE SUNDAE CAKE

2⅓ cups Gold Medal
  all-purpose flour*
1½ cups sugar
  1 teaspoon baking soda
  1 teaspoon salt
  ½ teaspoon baking powder
  ½ cup shortening
  ½ cup water
  ¾ cup buttermilk

  ½ cup chocolate syrup
  1 teaspoon vanilla
  2 eggs
  ½ cup chocolate syrup
    Chocolate Sundae Filling
    (below)
  1 tablespoon chocolate
    syrup

General Mills made history in 1943 with a streamlined method for making cakes. Featured in this 1944 advertisement, the new method cut mixing time in half. It used only one mixing bowl and eliminated creaming and separate beating of eggs. Dry ingredients were sifted together; then shortening and liquid were added.

In 1961 Gold Medal revolutionized cake-making again with the first "no-sift" flour. An advertisement that year described the flour as being "milled through sifters 97 times finer than yours...the only flour that promises success without sifting or altering recipes." Following the pre-sifted flour introduction, Gold Medal cake recipes were further streamlined. And today most Gold Medal cake recipes follow the one-step method for mixing dry and liquid ingredients.

Heat oven to 350°. Grease and flour rectangular pan, 13×9×2 inches, 12-cup bundt cake pan, 2 round pans, 9×1½ inches, or 3 round pans, 8×1½ inches. Beat all ingredients except ½ cup chocolate syrup, the Chocolate Sundae Filling and 1 tablespoon chocolate syrup in large mixer bowl on low speed, scraping bowl constantly, 30 seconds. Beat on medium speed, scraping bowl occasionally, 3 minutes. Reserve ½ cup of the batter; pour remaining batter into pan(s). Mix the remaining ½ cup chocolate syrup into reserved batter. Marble half the mixture into batter in each pan.

Bake until wooden pick inserted in center comes out clean, rectangular 40 minutes, bundt cake 50 to 55 minutes, 9-inch layers 35 minutes, 8-inch layers 25 minutes. Cool layers or bundt cake 10 minutes; remove from pan(s). Cool completely. Frost rectangular or fill and frost layers with Chocolate Sundae Filling and drizzle 1 tablespoon chocolate syrup over top. Or top slices of bundt cake with Chocolate Sundae Filling. Refrigerate any remaining cake.

*If using self-rising flour, omit baking soda, salt and baking powder.

Chocolate Sundae Filling

Beat 1 cup chilled whipping cream and ¼ cup chocolate syrup in chilled bowl until stiff.

COCOA FUDGE CAKE

1⅔ cups Gold Medal
    all-purpose flour*
1½ cups sugar
⅔ cup cocoa
1½ teaspoons baking soda
1 teaspoon salt
1½ cups buttermilk
½ cup shortening
2 eggs
1 teaspoon vanilla
    Chocolate Butter
    Frosting (below) or
    powdered sugar

Heat oven to 350°. Grease and flour rectangular pan, 13×9×2 inches, 2 round pans, 8 or 9×1½ inches, or 12-cup bundt cake pan. Beat all ingredients except frosting in large mixer bowl on low speed, scraping bowl constantly, 30 seconds. Beat on high speed, scraping bowl occasionally, 3 minutes. Pour into pan(s).

Bake until wooden pick inserted in center comes out clean, rectangular 35 to 40 minutes, layers 30 to 35 minutes, bundt cake 40 to 45 minutes. Cool layers or bundt cake 10 minutes; remove from pan(s). Cool completely. Frost rectangular or fill and frost layers with Chocolate Butter Frosting. Sprinkle bundt cake with powdered sugar.

*If using self-rising flour, decrease soda to ¾ teaspoon and omit salt.

Chocolate Butter Frosting

⅓ cup margarine or
    butter, softened
2 ounces melted unsweet-
    ened chocolate (cool)
2 cups powdered sugar
1½ teaspoons vanilla
    About 2 tablespoons
    milk

Mix margarine and chocolate. Mix in powdered sugar. Beat in vanilla and milk until smooth and of spreading consistency.

SOUR CREAM CHOCOLATE CAKE

2 cups Gold Medal
    all-purpose flour*
2 cups sugar
1 cup water
¾ cup dairy sour cream
¼ cup shortening
1¼ teaspoons baking soda
1 teaspoon salt
½ teaspoon baking powder
2 eggs
1 teaspoon vanilla
4 ounces melted unsweet-
    ened chocolate (cool)
    Chocolate Butter
    Frosting (above)

Heat oven to 350°. Grease and flour rectangular pan, 13×9×2 inches, or 2 round pans, 9×1½ inches. Beat all ingredients except frosting in large mixer bowl on low speed, scraping bowl constantly, 30 seconds. Beat on high speed, scraping bowl occasionally, 3 minutes. Pour into pan(s).

Bake until top springs back when touched lightly, rectangular 40 to 45 minutes, layers 30 to 35 minutes. Cool layers 10 minutes; remove from pans. Cool completely. Frost rectangular or fill and frost layers with Chocolate Butter Frosting.

*If using self-rising flour, decrease baking soda to ¼ teaspoon and omit salt and baking powder.

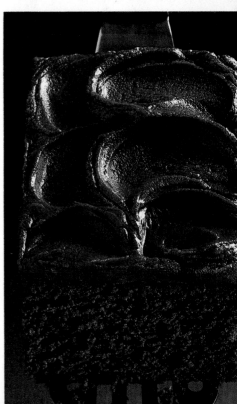

CHOCOLATE ROLL

¾ cup Gold Medal
   all-purpose flour*
¼ cup cocoa
1 teaspoon baking powder
¼ teaspoon salt
3 eggs
1 cup granulated sugar
⅓ cup water

1 teaspoon vanilla
   Powdered sugar
1 quart chocolate mint or
   vanilla ice cream, slightly
   softened
   French Silk Frosting
   (below)

Heat oven to 375°. Line jelly roll pan, 15½ × 10½ × 1 inch, with aluminum foil or waxed paper; grease. Mix flour, cocoa, baking powder and salt. Beat eggs in small mixer bowl until very thick and lemon colored, about 5 minutes. Pour eggs into large mixer bowl. Beat in granulated sugar gradually. Beat in water and vanilla on low speed. Mix in dry ingredients gradually, beating just until batter is smooth. Pour into pan, spreading batter to corners.

Bake until wooden pick inserted in center comes out clean, 12 to 15 minutes. Loosen cake from edges of pan; invert on towel sprinkled with powdered sugar. Carefully remove foil; trim off stiff edges if necessary. While hot, roll cake and towel from narrow end. Cool on wire rack. Unroll cake; remove towel. Spread with ice cream. Roll up; wrap in plastic wrap. Freeze until firm, about 6 hours. Frost with French Silk Frosting.   10 servings.

*If using self-rising flour, omit baking powder and salt.

French Silk Frosting

⅓ cup margarine or
   butter, softened
1⅓ cups powdered sugar

1 ounce melted unsweet-
   ened chocolate (cool)
½ teaspoon vanilla
1 tablespoon milk

Beat margarine, powdered sugar, chocolate and vanilla on low speed until blended. Gradually beat in milk until fluffy.

Chocolate-Almond Roll: Omit ice cream. Beat 1 cup chilled whipping cream, ¼ cup powdered sugar and 2 tablespoons cocoa in chilled bowl until stiff. Beat in ½ teaspoon vanilla. Fold in ¼ cup toasted sliced almonds. Spread roll with whipped cream mixture. Roll up; frost with French Silk Frosting. Refrigerate any remaining cake roll.

While hot, gently roll up the cake and towel. After cake is cool, unroll and remove towel.

BONNIE BUTTER CAKE

⅔ cup margarine or
   butter, softened
1¾ cups sugar
2 eggs
1½ teaspoons vanilla
2¾ cups Gold Medal
   all-purpose flour*

2½ teaspoons baking
   powder
1 teaspoon salt
1¼ cups milk
   Chocolate Butter
   Frosting (page 77)

Heat oven to 350°. Grease and flour rectangular pan, 13×9×2 inches, or 2 round pans, 9×1½ inches. Mix margarine, sugar, eggs and vanilla in large mixer bowl until fluffy. Beat on high speed, scraping bowl occasionally, 5 minutes. Beat in flour, baking powder and salt alternately with milk on low speed. Pour into pan(s).

Bake until wooden pick inserted in center comes out clean, rectangular 45 to 50 minutes, layers 30 to 35 minutes. Cool layers 10 minutes; remove from pans. Cool completely. Frost rectangular or fill and frost layers with Chocolate Butter Frosting.

*If using self-rising flour, omit baking powder and salt.

DINETTE CAKE

1¼ cups Gold Medal
   all-purpose flour*
1 cup sugar
1½ teaspoons baking
   powder
½ teaspoon salt

¾ cup milk
⅓ cup shortening
1 egg
1 teaspoon vanilla
   French Silk Frosting
   (opposite)

Heat oven to 350°. Grease and flour square pan, 8×8×2 or 9×9×2 inches, or round pan, 9×1½ inches. Beat all ingredients except frosting in large mixer bowl on low speed, scraping bowl constantly, 30 seconds. Beat on high speed, scraping bowl occasionally, 3 minutes. Pour into pan.

Bake until wooden pick inserted in center comes out clean, square 35 to 40 minutes, round 35 minutes; cool. Frost with French Silk Frosting.

*If using self-rising flour, omit baking powder and salt.

In the 1890s this popular cake was called a One-Egg Cake. During the 1920s and 1930s, it was promoted as the Emergency or Lazy Day Cake. A 1940 Gold Medal advertisement called it Busy Day Cake or a "foundation" cake which could be varied with flavorings and icings. Still popular in 1955, it was referred to as a Kitchenette Cake.

APPLESAUCE-SPICE CAKE

2½ cups Gold Medal all-purpose flour*	¼ teaspoon baking powder
2 cups sugar	1½ cups applesauce
1½ teaspoons baking soda	½ cup water
1½ teaspoons salt	½ cup shortening
¾ teaspoon ground cinnamon	2 eggs
½ teaspoon ground cloves	1 cup raisins
½ teaspoon ground allspice	½ cup chopped walnuts
	Browned Butter Frosting (below)

Heat oven to 350°. Grease and flour rectangular pan, 13×9×2 inches, or 2 round pans, 8 or 9×1½ inches. Beat all ingredients except frosting in large mixer bowl on low speed, scraping bowl constantly, 30 seconds. Beat on high speed, scraping bowl occasionally, 3 minutes. Pour into pan(s).

Bake until wooden pick inserted in center comes out clean, rectangular 60 to 65 minutes, layers 50 to 55 minutes. Cool layers 10 minutes; remove from pans. Cool completely. Frost rectangular or fill and frost layers with Browned Butter Frosting.

*Do not use self-rising flour in this recipe.

Browned Butter Frosting

Heat ⅓ cup margarine or butter over medium heat until delicate brown. Mix in 3 cups powdered sugar. Beat in 1½ teaspoons vanilla and about 2 tablespoons milk until smooth and of spreading consistency.

POUND CAKE

1¼ cups margarine or butter, softened	3 cups Gold Medal all-purpose flour*
2¾ cups sugar	1 teaspoon baking powder
5 eggs	¼ teaspoon salt
1 teaspoon vanilla	1 cup evaporated milk

Heat oven to 350°. Grease and flour tube pan, 10×4 inches, or 12-cup bundt cake pan. Beat margarine, sugar, eggs and vanilla in large mixer bowl on low speed, scraping bowl constantly, 30 seconds. Beat on high speed, scraping bowl occasionally, 5 minutes. Beat in flour, baking powder and salt alternately with milk on low speed. Pour into pan.

Bake until wooden pick inserted in center comes out clean, 70 to 80 minutes. Cool in pan about 20 minutes; remove from pan.

*Do not use self-rising flour in this recipe. ✤

*A*pplesauce Cake was one of the recipes contributed by world famous chefs to this handsome cookbook, Betty Crocker's $25,000 Recipe Set. Printed in France, the book was brought home on the Normandie's maiden voyage.

*I*n 1895 Sperry Flour Company produced a recipe booklet, Easy Cooking for Little Cooks. Sperry was one of the firms that joined General Mills, Inc.

Included in the booklet was a recipe for Pound Cake, given its name because the primary ingredients originally were one pound each butter, powdered sugar and sifted flour. With the recipes were drawings showing how to measure ingredients in the typical measuring utensils of the day...tableware teaspoons and coffee cups.

WILLIAMSBURG ORANGE CAKE

2½ cups Gold Medal
    all-purpose flour*
1½ cups sugar
1½ teaspoons baking soda
 ¾ teaspoon salt
1½ cups buttermilk
 ½ cup margarine or
    butter, softened
 ¼ cup shortening

3 eggs
1½ teaspoons vanilla
1 cup golden raisins, cut up
½ cup chopped nuts
1 tablespoon grated orange
   peel
Orange Butter Frosting
  (below)

Heat oven to 350°. Grease and flour rectangular pan, 13×9×2 inches, or 2 round pans, 9×1½ inches. Beat all ingredients except frosting in large mixer bowl on low speed, scraping bowl constantly, 30 seconds. Beat on high speed, scraping bowl occasionally, 3 minutes. Pour into pan(s).

Bake until wooden pick inserted in center comes out clean, rectangular 45 to 50 minutes, layers 30 to 35 minutes. Cool layers 10 minutes; remove from pans. Cool completely. Frost rectangular or fill and frost layers with Orange Butter Frosting.

*If using self-rising flour, decrease soda to ½ teaspoon and omit salt.

Orange Butter Frosting

Mix ⅓ cup margarine or butter, softened, and 3 cups powdered sugar. Beat in 2 teaspoons grated orange peel and about 2 tablespoons orange juice until of spreading consistency.

 SILVER WHITE CAKE

2¼	cups Gold Medal all-purpose flour*	1¼	cups milk
1⅔	cups sugar	1	teaspoon vanilla
3½	teaspoons baking powder	5	egg whites
1	teaspoon salt		Lemon Filling (below)
⅔	cup shortening		White Mountain Frosting (below)
		¼	cup flaked coconut

Heat oven to 350°. Grease and flour rectangular pan, 13×9×2 inches, or 2 round pans, 8 or 9×1½ inches. Beat flour, sugar, baking powder, salt, shortening, milk and vanilla in large mixer bowl on low speed, scraping bowl constantly, 30 seconds. Beat on high speed, scraping bowl occasionally, 2 minutes. Add egg whites; beat on high speed, scraping bowl occasionally, 2 minutes. Pour into pan(s).

Bake until wooden pick inserted in center comes out clean, rectangular 40 to 45 minutes, layers 30 to 35 minutes. Cool layers 10 minutes; remove from pans. Cool completely. Fill layers with Lemon Filling. Frost cake with White Mountain Frosting; sprinkle with coconut.

*If using self-rising flour, omit baking powder and salt. Do not use 8-inch layers.

Lemon Filling

¾	cup sugar	1	tablespoon margarine or butter
3	tablespoons cornstarch	⅓	cup lemon juice
¼	teaspoon salt	4	drops yellow food color, if desired
¾	cup water		
1	teaspoon grated lemon peel		

Mix sugar, cornstarch and salt in saucepan. Stir in water gradually. Cook, stirring constantly, until mixture thickens and boils. Boil and stir 5 minutes. Remove from heat; add lemon peel and margarine. Stir in lemon juice and food color; cool. If filling is too soft, refrigerate until set.

White Mountain Frosting

½	cup sugar	2	egg whites
¼	cup light corn syrup	1	teaspoon vanilla
2	tablespoons water		

Mix sugar, corn syrup and water in saucepan. Cover; heat to rolling boil over medium heat. Remove cover and boil rapidly to 242° on candy thermometer or until small amount of mixture dropped into very cold water forms a firm ball that holds its shape until pressed. As mixture boils, beat egg whites until stiff peaks form. Pour hot syrup very slowly in a thin stream into egg whites, beating constantly on medium speed. Add vanilla; beat on high speed until stiff peaks form.

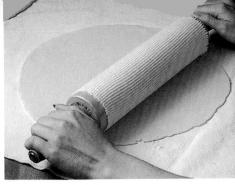

STANDARD PASTRY

9-inch One-Crust Pie	**9-inch Two-Crust Pie**
⅓ cup plus 1 tablespoon shortening or ⅓ cup lard	⅔ cup plus 2 tablespoons shortening or ⅔ cup lard
1 cup Gold Medal all-purpose flour*	2 cups Gold Medal all-purpose flour*
½ teaspoon salt	1 teaspoon salt
2 to 3 tablespoons cold water	4 to 5 tablespoons cold water

Cut shortening into flour and salt until particles are size of small peas. Sprinkle in water, 1 tablespoon at a time, tossing with fork until all flour is moistened and pastry almost cleans side of bowl (1 to 2 teaspoons water can be added if necessary).

Gather pastry into a ball; shape into flattened round on lightly floured cloth-covered board. (For Two-Crust Pie, divide pastry into halves and shape into 2 rounds.) Roll pastry 2 inches larger than inverted pie plate with floured stockinet-covered rolling pin. Fold pastry into quarters; place in plate. Unfold and ease into plate, pressing firmly against bottom and side.

For One-Crust Pie: Trim overhanging edge of pastry 1 inch from rim of plate. Fold and roll pastry under, even with plate; flute. Fill and bake as directed in recipe.

For Baked Pie Shell: Prick bottom and side thoroughly with fork. Bake in 475° oven until light brown, 8 to 10 minutes; cool.

For Two-Crust Pie: Turn desired filling into pastry-lined pie plate. Trim overhanging edge of pastry ½ inch from rim of plate. Roll other round of pastry. Fold into quarters; cut slits so steam can escape. Place over filling and unfold. Trim overhanging edge of pastry 1 inch from rim of plate. Fold and roll top edge under lower edge, pressing on rim to seal; flute. Cover edge with 2- to 3-inch strip of aluminum foil to prevent excessive browning; remove foil during last 15 minutes of baking. Bake as directed in recipe.

*If using self-rising flour, omit salt. Pie crusts made with self-rising flour differ in flavor and texture from those made with all-purpose flour.

Nut Pastry: Stir 2 tablespoons finely chopped nuts into flour for One-Crust Pie; use ¼ cup finely chopped nuts for Two-Crust Pie.

Roll pastry lightly, working from the center to the outer edge. Roll evenly in all directions but not back and forth. Lift rolling pin at edge to keep pastry from becoming too thin.

Roll pastry 2 inches larger than inverted pie plate. Patch dough by lightly moistening the tear and a strip from the pastry edge; press together. Roll to seal.

One-Crust Pie: Fold and roll top pastry edge under the lower edge inside the plate rim. Pinch firmly to seal. Flute as desired.

Berry pies, featured in this 1943 Gold Medal advertisement, can be traced back more than 350 years. New England colonists made blueberry and raspberry pies. The Pennsylvania Dutch settlers used currants, blackberries, elderberries and gooseberries.

Center first strip; space others equally on either side. Fold back every other one of the original strips; weave cross-strips, handling the center one first.

BERRY PIE

Lattice Top (below)	4 cups fresh berries
1 cup sugar	(raspberries, black-
⅓ cup Gold Medal	berries, boysenberries)
all-purpose flour*	2 tablespoons margarine
	or butter
	Milk

Heat oven to 425°. Prepare Lattice Top. Mix sugar and flour; gently stir in berries. Turn into pastry-lined pie plate; dot with margarine. Arrange pastry strips on filling as directed; trim ends. Seal and flute, building up high edge. Brush pastry with milk; sprinkle with sugar if desired. Cover edge with 2- to 3-inch strip of aluminum foil to prevent excessive browning; remove foil during last 15 minutes of baking. Bake until crust is golden brown, 35 to 45 minutes.

*Self-rising flour can be used in this recipe.

Lattice Top

Prepare Pastry for 9-inch Two-Crust Pie (page 85) as directed except—leave 1 inch overhang on lower crust. After rolling pastry for top crust, cut into 10 strips, about ½ inch wide. (Pastry wheel can be used for more decorative strips.) Place 5 strips across filling. Weave a cross-strip through center by first folding back every other strip going the other way. Continue weaving until lattice is complete, folding back alternate strips each time cross-strip is added.

Blueberry Pie: Decrease sugar to ½ cup, add ½ teaspoon ground cinnamon and use 4 cups fresh blueberries. Sprinkle blueberries with 1 tablespoon lemon juice before dotting with margarine.

CRANBERRY-APPLE PIE

Pastry for 9-inch	3 cups sliced pared tart
Two-Crust Pie (page 85)	apples (about 3
1¾ cups sugar	medium)
¼ cup Gold Medal	2 cups fresh or frozen
all-purpose flour*	(thawed) cranberries
	2 tablespoons margarine
	or butter

Heat oven to 425°. Prepare pastry. Mix sugar and flour. Alternate layers of apples, cranberries and sugar mixture in pastry-lined pie plate, beginning and ending with apples. Dot with margarine. Cover with top crust that has slits cut in it; seal and flute. Cover edge with 2- to 3-inch strip of aluminum foil to prevent excessive browning; remove foil during last 15 minutes of baking. Bake until crust is golden brown and juice begins to bubble through slits in crust, 40 to 50 minutes.

*Self-rising flour can be used in this recipe.

86

APPLESCOTCH PIE

5 cups thinly sliced pared
   tart apples
   (about 5 medium)
1 cup packed brown sugar
¼ cup water
1 tablespoon lemon juice
¼ cup Gold Medal
   all-purpose flour*

2 tablespoons granulated
   sugar
¾ teaspoon salt
1 teaspoon vanilla
3 tablespoons margarine
   or butter
   Pastry for 9-inch
   Two-Crust Pie (page 85)

Mix apples, brown sugar, water and lemon juice in 2-quart saucepan. Heat to boiling; reduce heat. Cover and simmer just until apples are tender, 7 to 8 minutes. Mix flour, granulated sugar and salt; stir into apple mixture. Cook, stirring constantly, until mixture thickens and boils. Boil and stir 1 minute; remove from heat. Stir in vanilla and margarine; cool.

Heat oven to 425°. Prepare pastry. Turn apple mixture into pastry-lined pie plate. Cover with top crust that has slits cut in it; seal and flute. Cover edge with 2- to 3-inch strip of aluminum foil to prevent excessive browning; remove foil during last 15 minutes of baking. Bake until crust is golden brown, 40 to 45 minutes.

*Self-rising flour can be used in this recipe.

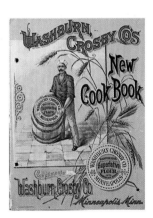

The round, flat apple pie featured in *Washburn Crosby Co.'s New Cook Book* of 1894 is an American classic. This pie shape was created by thrifty American colonists so that "a little would go a long way." Apple "pye" of old England was made in a long, deep dish called a "coffin."

MAPLE APPLE PIE

Pastry for 9-inch
Two-Crust Pie (page 85)
6 cups thinly sliced pared tart
apples (about 5 medium)
½ cup packed brown sugar

3 tablespoons margarine
or butter, melted
6 tablespoons maple-
flavored syrup

Heat oven to 425°. Prepare pastry. Mix apple slices and brown sugar. Turn into pastry-lined pie plate; drizzle with margarine and 3 tablespoons of the syrup. Cover with top crust that has slits cut in it; seal and flute. Bake 15 minutes. Make diagonal cuts about 1 inch apart through top crust. Make diagonal cuts crosswise through first cuts, creating diamond pattern. Pour remaining syrup over top. Cover edge with 2- to 3-inch strip of aluminum foil to prevent excessive browning. Bake until crust is deep golden brown, about 25 minutes.

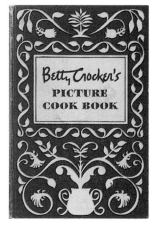

The *Betty Crocker's Picture Cook Book* of 1950 sold a million copies in its first year, establishing an all-time record in the book trade for a non-fiction best-seller. There have been four revised editions, with sales totaling 22 million.

Cut diamond pattern on partially baked top crust by making cuts about 1 inch apart through crust. Make diagonal cuts crosswise through first cuts. Pour remaining syrup over top.

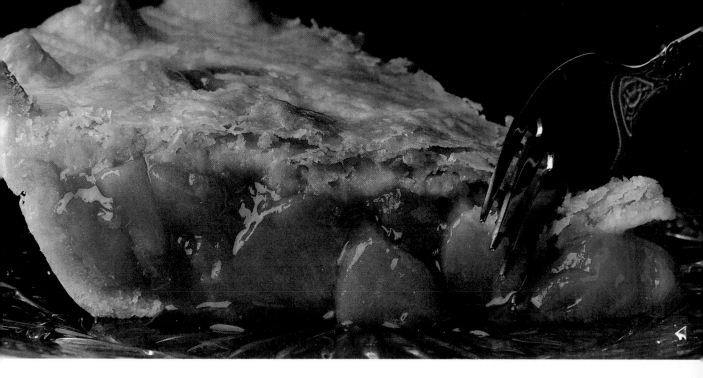

BLUSHING PEACH PIE

Pastry for 9-inch
Two-Crust Pie (page 85)
2 cans (29 ounces each)
sliced peaches, drained
½ cup sugar

¼ cup Gold Medal
all-purpose flour*
¼ cup red cinnamon candies
2 tablespoons margarine
or butter

Heat oven to 425°. Prepare pastry. Mix peaches, sugar, flour and candies; turn into pastry-lined pie plate. Dot with margarine. Cover with top crust that has slits cut in it; seal and flute. Cover edge with 2- to 3-inch strip of aluminum foil to prevent excessive browning; remove foil during last 15 minutes of baking. Bake until crust is golden brown and juice begins to bubble through slits in crust, 40 to 50 minutes.

*Self-rising flour can be used in this recipe.

SPICY WALNUT-RAISIN PIE

Pastry for 9-inch
One-Crust Pie (page 85)
3 eggs
⅔ cup sugar
½ teaspoon salt
½ teaspoon ground
cinnamon
½ teaspoon ground nutmeg

½ teaspoon ground cloves
1 cup light or dark corn syrup
⅓ cup margarine or
butter, melted
½ cup coarsely chopped
walnuts
½ cup raisins

Heat oven to 375°. Prepare pastry. Beat eggs, sugar, salt, cinnamon, nutmeg, cloves, corn syrup and margarine with hand beater until blended. Stir in walnuts and raisins. Pour into pastry-lined pie plate. Bake until set, 40 to 50 minutes.

STRAWBERRY GLACÉ PIE

9-inch Baked Pie Shell (page 85)
6 cups strawberries (about 1½ quarts)
1 cup sugar
3 tablespoons cornstarch
½ cup water
1 package (3 ounces) cream cheese, softened

Bake pie shell. Mash enough strawberries to measure 1 cup. Mix sugar and cornstarch in 2-quart saucepan. Stir in water and mashed strawberries gradually. Cook over medium heat, stirring constantly, until mixture thickens and boils. Boil and stir 1 minute; cool.

Beat cream cheese until smooth; spread on bottom of pie shell. Fill shell with whole strawberries; pour cooked strawberry mixture over top. Refrigerate until set, at least 3 hours.

Peach Glacé Pie: Substitute 5 cups sliced peaches (7 medium) for the strawberries. To prevent discoloration, use an ascorbic acid mixture as directed on package.

Raspberry Glacé Pie: Substitute raspberries for the strawberries.

Gold Medal went "strawberry wild" with this advertisement of 1961. The recipes for Strawberry Glacé Pie and four other luscious strawberry concoctions were included in sacks of Gold Medal flour.

SOUR CREAM-RAISIN MERINGUE PIE

9-inch Baked Pie Shell
(page 85)
1 tablespoon plus 1½
teaspoons cornstarch
1 cup plus 2 tablespoons
sugar
¼ teaspoon salt

¾ teaspoon ground nutmeg
1½ cups dairy sour cream
3 egg yolks
1½ cups raisins
1 tablespoon lemon juice
Brown Sugar Meringue
(below)

Bake pie shell. Reduce oven temperature to 400°. Mix cornstarch, sugar, salt and nutmeg in 2-quart saucepan. Stir in sour cream. Stir in egg yolks, raisins and lemon juice. Cook over medium heat, stirring constantly, until mixture thickens and boils. Boil and stir 1 minute. Pour into pie shell.

Spoon Brown Sugar Meringue onto hot pie filling; spread over filling, sealing meringue to edge of crust to prevent shrinking or weeping. Bake until delicate brown, about 10 minutes. Cool away from draft.

Brown Sugar Meringue

Beat 3 egg whites and ¼ teaspoon cream of tartar until foamy. Beat in 6 tablespoons brown sugar, 1 tablespoon at a time; continue beating until stiff and glossy. Do not underbeat. Beat in ½ teaspoon vanilla.

In 1950 Gold Medal introduced the new and easy Stir-N-Roll Pastry method. Liquid shortening, which replaced the solid shortening traditionally used for pies, was combined with other liquid ingredients and poured all at once into the dry ingredient mixture. Stir-N-Roll Biscuits, introduced in 1951, used the same mixing technique as did Stir-N-Roll Crescents, promoted in 1953.

COLONIAL INNKEEPER'S PIE

Pastry for 9-inch
  One-Crust Pie (page 85)
½ bar (4-ounce size) sweet
  cooking chocolate
½ cup water
⅔ cup sugar
¼ cup margarine
  or butter
1½ teaspoons vanilla

1 cup Gold Medal
  all-purpose flour*
¾ cup sugar
1 teaspoon baking powder
½ teaspoon salt
¼ cup shortening
½ cup milk
½ teaspoon vanilla
1 egg
½ cup finely chopped nuts

Heat oven to 350°. Prepare pastry. Heat chocolate and water over low heat until melted. Add ⅔ cup sugar. Heat to boiling, stirring constantly; remove from heat. Stir in margarine and 1½ teaspoons vanilla (chocolate mixture will be thin).

Beat remaining ingredients except egg and nuts in small mixer bowl on low speed until blended. Beat on medium speed, scraping bowl constantly, 2 minutes. Add egg; beat, scraping bowl frequently, 2 minutes longer. Pour into pastry-lined pie plate. Stir chocolate mixture; pour over mixture in pie plate. Sprinkle with nuts. Bake until wooden pick inserted in center comes out clean, 55 to 60 minutes. Serve with sweetened whipped cream if desired.

*Do not use self-rising flour in this recipe.

PUMPKIN-CHEESE PIE

Pastry for 9-inch
  One-Crust Pie (page 85)
1 package (8 ounces) cream
  cheese, softened
¾ cup sugar
2 tablespoons Gold Medal
  all-purpose flour*
1 teaspoon ground
  cinnamon
¼ teaspoon ground nutmeg

¼ teaspoon ground ginger
1 teaspoon grated
  lemon peel
1 teaspoon grated
  orange peel
¼ teaspoon vanilla
3 eggs
1 can (16 ounces) pumpkin
Sour Cream Topping
  (below)

Heat oven to 350°. Prepare pastry. Beat cream cheese, sugar and flour in large mixer bowl until blended. Add remaining ingredients except topping; beat on medium speed until smooth. Pour into pastry-lined pie plate. Bake until knife inserted in center comes out clean, 50 to 55 minutes. Immediately spread with Sour Cream Topping; cool. Refrigerate at least 4 hours.

*Self-rising flour can be used in this recipe.

Sour Cream Topping

Mix ¾ cup dairy sour cream, 1 tablespoon sugar and ¼ teaspoon vanilla.

LEMON CAKE PIE

Pastry for 9-inch
  One-Crust Pie (page 85)
3 eggs, separated
2 tablespoons grated
  lemon peel
⅔ cup lemon juice
1 cup milk
1¼ cups sugar
⅓ cup Gold Medal
  all-purpose flour*
¼ teaspoon salt

Heat oven to 350°. Prepare pastry. Beat egg whites in large mixer bowl until stiff peaks form; reserve. Beat egg yolks; beat in lemon peel, lemon juice and milk. Add sugar, flour and salt; beat until smooth. Beat lemon mixture into egg whites on low speed until blended, about 1 minute. Pour into pastry-lined pie plate. Bake until golden brown, 45 to 50 minutes. Serve with sweetened whipped cream if desired.

*Do not use self-rising flour in this recipe.

FROSTY FRUIT PIE

9-inch Baked Pie Shell
  (page 85)
1 can (13 ounces)
  evaporated milk
1 can (8¼ ounces) crushed
  pineapple
1 package (3 ounces)
  lemon-flavored gelatin
¾ cup sugar
2 tablespoons lemon juice

Bake pie shell. Pour evaporated milk into baking pan, 8×8×2 inches. Freeze until soft ice crystals form around edges of pan, about 25 minutes. Heat pineapple (with syrup) to boiling. Stir in gelatin and sugar until dissolved. Refrigerate in large mixer bowl until set but not firm, about 1 hour.

Beat chilled evaporated milk in small mixer bowl until stiff, about 2 minutes. Add lemon juice; beat until very stiff, 1 to 2 minutes. Beat into gelatin mixture on low speed until blended, about 1 minute. Spoon into pie shell. Refrigerate until firm, at least 4 hours. Serve with sweetened whipped cream and garnish with mint leaves if desired.

CHOCOLATE PIE DELUXE

9-inch Baked Pie Shell (page 85)
1½ cups miniature marshmallows or 16 large marshmallows

½ cup milk
1 bar (8 ounces) milk chocolate candy
1 cup chilled whipping cream

Bake pie shell. Heat marshmallows, milk and chocolate over low heat, stirring constantly, just until chocolate and marshmallows are melted and mixture is smooth. Refrigerate, stirring occasionally, until mixture mounds slightly when dropped from a spoon.

Beat whipping cream in chilled bowl until stiff. Fold chocolate mixture into whipped cream. Pour into pie shell. Refrigerate until set, about 8 hours. Spread with sweetened whipped cream and garnish with chocolate curls if desired. 8 to 10 servings.

Make chocolate curls by gently pulling vegetable parer across top of sweetened chocolate bar.

CHOCOLATE BROWNIE PIE

Pastry for 9-inch
   One-Crust Pie (page 85)
2 squares (1 ounce each)
   unsweetened chocolate
2 tablespoons margarine
   or butter

3 eggs
½ cup sugar
¾ cup dark corn syrup
1 cup pecan halves

Heat oven to 375°. Prepare pastry. Heat chocolate and margarine over low heat until melted; cool. Beat chocolate mixture, eggs, sugar and corn syrup with hand beater. Stir in pecans. Pour into pastry-lined pie plate. Bake just until set, 40 to 50 minutes. Serve with sweetened whipped cream if desired.

BANANA CREAM PIE

9-inch Baked Pie Shell
   (page 85)
3 medium bananas
1 package (8 ounces) cream
   cheese, softened

1 can (14 ounces)
   sweetened condensed
   milk
⅓ cup lemon juice
1 teaspoon vanilla

Bake pie shell. Slice 2 of the bananas; arrange in pie shell. Beat cream cheese in small mixer bowl on medium speed until light and fluffy. Gradually beat in milk until well blended. Beat in lemon juice and vanilla. Pour into pie shell. Refrigerate until firm, at least 2 hours. Slice remaining banana; arrange on pie.

This Gold Medal advertisement of 1953 introduced the new Chocolate Brownie Pie which was like a pecan pie and brownies all in one great taste.

Fill cookie cutouts with crushed candy or whole candy, depending on size and shape of design.

MAGIC WINDOW COOKIES *(pictured on pages 96-97)*

1 cup sugar	1 teaspoon baking powder
¾ cup shortening (part margarine or butter, softened)	1 teaspoon salt
2 eggs	About 5 rolls (about .79 ounce each) ring-shaped hard candy (wild cherry, tangerine, fancy fruits, five flavor, butter rum or butterscotch)
1 teaspoon vanilla or ½ teaspoon lemon extract	
2½ cups Gold Medal all-purpose flour*	

Mix sugar, shortening, eggs and vanilla. Stir in flour, baking powder and salt. Cover and refrigerate at least 1 hour.

Heat oven to 375°. Roll dough ⅛ inch thick on lightly floured cloth-covered board. Cut into desired shapes, using cutters of 2 sizes to obtain cutouts, or design your own patterns. Place cookies on aluminum foil-covered cookie sheet. (For larger cookies, transfer to cookie sheet before cutting out designs.) Place partially crushed (place between paper towels and tap lightly) or whole candy in cutouts, depending on size and shape of design. If cookies are to be hung, make a hole in each ¼ inch from top with end of plastic straw.

Bake until cookies are very light brown and candy is melted, 7 to 9 minutes. If candy has not spread within cutout design, immediately spread with metal spatula. Cool completely on cookie sheet. Gently remove cookies.

About 6 dozen 3-inch cookies.

*If using self-rising flour, omit baking powder and salt.

PETITE PEPPERNUTS

¾ cup packed brown sugar	½ teaspoon baking soda
½ cup shortening	½ teaspoon ground cinnamon
1 egg	
½ cup light molasses	½ teaspoon ground cloves
3 drops anise oil	¼ teaspoon salt
1 tablespoon hot water	⅛ teaspoon white pepper
3⅓ cups Gold Medal all-purpose flour*	

Mix brown sugar, shortening, egg, molasses, anise oil and water. Stir in remaining ingredients. Knead dough until right consistency for molding. Shape dough into rolls, ½ inch in diameter. Wrap and refrigerate until firm, at least 2 hours.

Heat oven to 350°. Cut rolls into ¼-inch slices; place slightly apart on ungreased cookie sheet. Bake until set and golden brown on bottoms, about 9 minutes. Store in airtight container.

About 35 dozen cookies.

*If using self-rising flour, omit baking soda and salt.

Molded Peppernuts: After kneading, shape dough into ¾-inch balls. Place about 1 inch apart on ungreased cookie sheet. Bake until golden brown, about 12 minutes. About 11 dozen cookies.

PAINTBRUSH COOKIES

1½ cups powdered sugar
 1 cup margarine or
    butter, softened
 1 egg
 1 teaspoon vanilla
 ½ teaspoon almond extract

2½ cups Gold Medal
    all-purpose flour*
 1 teaspoon baking soda
 1 teaspoon cream of tartar
    Egg Yolk Paint (below)

Mix powdered sugar, margarine, egg, vanilla and almond extract. Stir in flour, baking soda and cream of tartar. Cover and refrigerate 2 to 3 hours.

Heat oven to 375°. Divide dough into halves. Roll each half 3/16 inch thick on lightly floured cloth-covered board. Cut into desired shapes with cookie cutters. Place on lightly greased cookie sheet. Prepare Egg Yolk Paint; paint designs on cookies with small paintbrushes. Bake until edges are light brown, 7 to 8 minutes.

About 5 dozen 2- to 2½-inch cookies.

*If using self-rising flour, omit baking soda and cream of tartar.

Egg Yolk Paint

Mix 1 egg yolk and ¼ teaspoon water. Divide mixture among several small custard cups. Tint each with different food color to make bright colors. If paint thickens while standing, stir in few drops water.

Paint designs or monograms on unbaked cookies with paintbrushes.

CHOCOLATE PEPPERMINT COOKIE TWISTS

½ cup margarine or
    butter, softened
½ cup shortening
1 cup powdered sugar
1 egg
1½ teaspoons vanilla

2½ cups Gold Medal
    all-purpose flour
½ cup cocoa
1 teaspoon salt
Chocolate Glaze (below)
¼ cup crushed peppermint
    candy

Roll dough into pencil-like, 9-inch strips; place on cookie sheet. Twist into pretzel shape.

Heat oven to 375°. Mix margarine, shortening, powdered sugar, egg and vanilla. Stir in flour, cocoa and salt. Knead level tablespoonful of dough with hands until right consistency for molding. Roll into pencil-like strip, about 9 inches long, on lightly floured board. Twist into pretzel shape on ungreased cookie sheet. Repeat with remaining dough. Bake until set, about 9 minutes. Let stand 1 to 2 minutes before removing from cookie sheet; cool. Dip tops of cookies into Chocolate Glaze. Sprinkle with peppermint candy.

About 4 dozen cookies.

Chocolate Glaze

Heat 2 squares (1 ounce each) unsweetened chocolate and 2 tablespoons margarine or butter over low heat until melted; remove from heat. Beat in 2 cups powdered sugar and 3 to 4 tablespoons water until smooth and of desired consistency.

DELUXE CHOCOLATE BARS

⅓ cup margarine or
    butter, softened
½ cup packed brown sugar
1 cup Gold Medal
    all-purpose flour
2 eggs, beaten
1 cup packed brown sugar
1 teaspoon vanilla

2 tablespoons Gold Medal
    all-purpose flour
1 teaspoon baking powder
½ teaspoon salt
1 package (6 ounces)
    semisweet chocolate
    chips
1 cup chopped nuts
Chocolate Glaze (below)

Heat oven to 350°. Mix ⅓ cup margarine and ½ cup brown sugar. Stir in 1 cup flour. Press in ungreased baking pan, 13×9×2 inches. Bake 10 minutes.

Mix eggs, 1 cup brown sugar and the vanilla. Stir in flour, baking powder and salt. Mix in chocolate chips and nuts; spread over baked layer. Bake until golden brown, 15 to 20 minutes. Cool; drizzle with Chocolate Glaze. Refrigerate until firm, about 1½ hours. Cut into bars, about 2×1½ inches.   3 dozen cookies.

Chocolate Glaze

Mix 1 tablespoon plus 1½ teaspoons cocoa, 1 tablespoon plus 1 teaspoon margarine or butter and 2 tablespoons boiling water in saucepan. Cook over low heat, stirring occasionally until thick and smooth; remove from heat. Beat in 1 cup powdered sugar until smooth.

Top: Chocolate Peppermint Cookie Twists, Candy Cane Cookies. Bottom: Deluxe Chocolate Bars, Mincemeat Bars.

Press 1 red and 1 white 4-inch strip of dough together lightly. Twist by turning ends in opposite directions.

CANDY CANE COOKIES

1 cup powdered sugar	2½ cups Gold Medal all-purpose flour*
½ cup margarine or butter, softened	1 teaspoon salt
½ cup shortening	½ teaspoon red food color
1 egg	½ cup crushed peppermint candy
1½ teaspoons almond or peppermint extract	½ cup granulated sugar
1 teaspoon vanilla	

Heat oven to 375°. Mix powdered sugar, margarine, shortening, egg, almond extract and vanilla. Stir in flour and salt. Divide dough into halves. Tint 1 half with food color.

For each candy cane, shape 1 teaspoon dough from each part into 4-inch rope. For smooth, even strips, roll back and forth on lightly floured board. Place 1 red and 1 white strip side by side; press together lightly and twist. Complete cookies 1 at a time. Place on ungreased cookie sheet. Curve top down to form handle of cane. Bake until set and very light brown, about 9 minutes. Mix candy and granulated sugar; immediately sprinkle over cookies. Remove from cookie sheet.   About 4 dozen cookies.

*If using self-rising flour, omit salt.

MINCEMEAT BARS

½ cup margarine or butter, softened	½ teaspoon baking soda
¼ cup shortening	1 cup quick-cooking oats
1 cup packed brown sugar	1 jar (28 ounces) prepared mincemeat
1½ cups Gold Medal all-purpose flour	½ cup chopped walnuts or almonds
1 teaspoon salt	

Heat oven to 400°. Grease baking pan, 13×9×2 inches. Mix margarine, shortening and brown sugar. Stir in flour, salt, baking soda and oats. Press half of the crumbly mixture in pan. Mix mincemeat and walnuts; spread over top. Sprinkle with remaining crumbly mixture, pressing lightly. Bake until light brown, 25 to 30 minutes. While warm, make 1 diagonal cut from corner to corner. Continue cutting parallel to first cut, each about 1½ inches apart. Repeat, cutting diagonally in opposite direction.
                    About 40 cookies.

Date-Apricot Bars: Mix 1¼ cups cut-up dates, 1½ cups cut-up dried apricots, ½ cup sugar and 1½ cups water in saucepan. Cook over medium-low heat, stirring constantly, until thickened, about 10 minutes. Substitute date-apricot filling for the mincemeat filling.

Date-Raisin Bars: Mix 1½ cups cut-up dates, 1½ cups raisins, ¼ cup sugar and 1½ cups water in saucepan. Cook over low heat, stirring constantly, until thickened, about 10 minutes. Substitute date-raisin filling for the mincemeat filling.

CANDY CANE COFFEE CAKE

2 cups dairy sour cream
2 packages active dry yeast
½ cup warm water
(105 to 115°)
¼ cup margarine or
butter, softened
⅓ cup sugar
2 teaspoons salt
2 eggs

About 6 cups Gold Medal
all-purpose flour
1½ cups snipped dried
apricots
1½ cups chopped drained
maraschino cherries
Margarine or butter,
softened
Glaze (below)

Heat sour cream over *low* heat *just* until lukewarm. Dissolve yeast in warm water in large mixing bowl. Add warm sour cream, ¼ cup margarine, the sugar, salt, eggs and 2 cups of the flour. Beat until smooth. Mix in enough remaining flour to make dough easy to handle.

Turn dough onto well-floured surface; knead until smooth and elastic, about 10 minutes. Place in greased bowl; turn greased side up. Cover; let rise in warm place until double, about 1 hour. (Dough is ready if indentation remains when touched.)

Heat oven to 375°. Punch down dough; divide into 3 equal parts. Roll each part into rectangle, 15×6 inches. Place on greased cookie sheet. Make 2-inch cuts on 15-inch sides of rectangles at ½-inch intervals. Mix apricots and cherries. Spread ⅓ of the fruit mixture lengthwise down center of each rectangle. Crisscross strips over fruit mixture. Stretch each rectangle to 22 inches; curve to form cane. Bake until golden brown, 15 to 20 minutes. Brush with margarine and drizzle with Glaze while warm. Decorate with cherry halves if desired.   3 coffee cakes.

Glaze

Mix 2 cups powdered sugar and about 2 tablespoons water. Beat in additional water, if necessary, until of desired consistency.

STOLLEN

1 package active dry yeast	½ cup chopped blanched almonds
¾ cup warm water (105 to 115°)	¼ cup cut-up citron
½ cup sugar	¼ cup cut-up candied cherries, if desired (not traditional)
½ teaspoon salt	
3 eggs	¼ cup raisins
1 egg, separated	1 tablespoon grated lemon peel
½ cup margarine or butter, softened	
3½ cups Gold Medal all-purpose flour*	Margarine or butter, softened
	1 tablespoon water

BE SURE YOUR BREAD IS MADE FROM GOLD MEDAL FLOUR

Dissolve yeast in ¾ cup warm water in large mixer bowl. Beat in sugar, salt, eggs, egg yolk, ½ cup margarine and 1¾ cups of the flour on medium speed, scraping bowl constantly, 10 minutes. Stir in remaining flour, the almonds, fruit and lemon peel. Scrape batter from side of bowl. Cover; let rise in warm place until double, 1½ to 2 hours.

Stir down batter by beating about 25 strokes. Cover tightly and store in refrigerator overnight.

Turn dough onto well-floured surface; turn to coat with flour. Divide into halves; press each half into oval, 10×7 inches. Spread with margarine. Fold lengthwise in half; press only folded edge firmly. Place on greased cookie sheet. Beat egg white and 1 tablespoon water; brush over ovals. Let rise until double, 45 to 60 minutes.

Heat oven to 375°. Bake until golden brown, 20 to 25 minutes. Sprinkle with powdered sugar if desired.   2 coffee cakes.

*Do not use self-rising flour in this recipe.

*A*mong the earliest holiday advertisements from Gold Medal was this one in 1919. The Kris Kringle Stollen recipe on this page was featured during the 1932 holidays and was offered free in Gold Medal flour bags. In 1942 a "Military" Christmas Cookies advertisement provided a recipe and patterns for making cookies in such forms as planes, ships and sailors. Candy Cane Cookies and Magic Window Cookies, both included in this section, were among the Gold Medal recipes offered in holiday advertisements of later years.

STEAMED PLUM PUDDING

1 cup milk	2 teaspoons ground
3 cups soft bread crumbs	cinnamon
½ cup shortening, melted	¼ teaspoon ground allspice
½ cup light molasses	¼ teaspoon ground cloves
1 cup Gold Medal	½ cup raisins
all-purpose flour*	½ cup snipped citron
1 teaspoon baking soda	Amber Sauce or Sherried
1 teaspoon salt	Hard Sauce (below)

Generously grease 4-cup mold. Pour milk over bread crumbs. Mix in shortening and molasses. Stir in remaining ingredients except Amber Sauce. Pour into mold; cover with aluminum foil.

Place mold on rack in Dutch oven; pour in boiling water to level of rack. Cover; heat to boiling. Keep water boiling over low heat to steam pudding until wooden pick inserted in center comes out clean, about 3 hours. (If necessary to add water during steaming, lift lid and quickly add boiling water.) Unmold and cut into slices. Serve with Amber Sauce.   6 to 8 servings.

*If using self-rising flour, decrease soda to ½ teaspoon and omit salt.

Amber Sauce

Mix 1 cup packed brown sugar or granulated sugar, ½ cup light corn syrup, ¼ cup margarine or butter and ½ cup half-and-half in saucepan. Cook over low heat, stirring occasionally, 5 minutes.

Sherried Hard Sauce

Beat ½ cup margarine or butter, softened, in small mixer bowl until creamy, fluffy and light in color, about 5 minutes. Gradually beat in 1 cup powdered sugar until smooth. Blend in 1 tablespoon sherry or brandy. Refrigerate until chilled, about 1 hour.

¶In 1922 Washburn Crosby began regularly highlighting recipes or specific foods in advertisements. During the holidays that year, this Christmas Plum Pudding advertisement appeared in the Saturday Evening Post. Gold Medal advertisements of the late 1940s and early 1950s encouraged homemakers to say "Happy Holidays" with gifts of plum pudding and other baked foods. Plum Pudding also was included in many company cookbooks, beginning with Miss Parloa's New Cook Book of 1880.

DELUXE OLD-FASHIONED FRUITCAKE

3 cups Gold Medal all-purpose flour*	1 package (15 ounces) golden raisins (about 3 cups)
1⅓ cups sugar	
2 teaspoons salt	1 package (8 ounces) pitted dates, cut into halves (1½ cups)
1 teaspoon baking powder	
2 teaspoons ground cinnamon	
1 teaspoon ground nutmeg	⅓ pound whole red and green candied cherries (¾ cup)
1 cup orange juice	
1 cup vegetable oil	⅓ pound red and green candied pineapple, cut up (about 1 cup)
4 eggs	
¼ cup dark molasses	
	½ pound whole Brazil nuts (1⅔ cups)

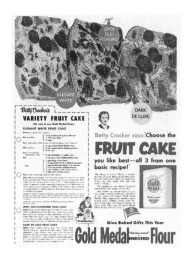

Heat oven to 275°. Line 2 baking pans, 9×5×3 or 8½×4½×2½ inches, with aluminum foil; grease. Beat all ingredients except fruits and nuts in large mixer bowl on low speed, scraping bowl constantly, 30 seconds. Beat on medium speed, scraping bowl occasionally, 3 minutes. Stir in fruits and nuts. Spread in pans. Bake until wooden pick inserted in center comes out clean, 2½ to 3 hours. If necessary, cover with aluminum foil during last hour of baking to prevent excessive browning. Remove from pans; cool. Wrap in plastic wrap or aluminum foil; store in cool place. Drizzle with Sweet Glaze (below) if desired.

*Do not use self-rising flour in this recipe.

Sweet Glaze

Heat 2 tablespoons light corn syrup and 1 tablespoon water just to rolling boil; cool to lukewarm.

This 1952 holiday advertisement for Gold Medal featured a recipe that could be varied to make three fruitcakes...white, dark and the old-fashioned style included here.

Holiday promotions of earlier years — during World War I and II and the depression — offered especially thrifty fruitcake recipes. Some did not include the candied fruits and dates. Others were called "economy" cakes because they were eggless, milkless and butterless.

KUGELHUPF

1 package active dry yeast	3 eggs
¼ cup warm water (105 to 115°)	2¾ cups Gold Medal all-purpose flour*
½ cup lukewarm milk (scalded then cooled)	½ cup golden raisins Grated peel of 1 lemon
½ cup sugar	⅓ cup very finely chopped almonds or dry bread crumbs
½ cup margarine or butter, softened	
½ teaspoon salt	12 to 16 whole blanched almonds

Dissolve yeast in warm water in large mixer bowl. Beat in milk, sugar, margarine, salt, eggs and 1¼ cups of the flour on low speed, scraping bowl constantly, 30 seconds. Beat on medium speed, scraping bowl occasionally, 4 minutes. Stir in raisins, lemon peel and the remaining flour. Scrape batter from side of bowl. Cover; let rise in warm place until double, about 1½ hours.

Grease bottom and side of 9-cup bundt cake pan or anodized aluminum ring mold; sprinkle with chopped almonds. Arrange whole almonds evenly in bottom of pan. Stir down batter by beating about 25 strokes. Spoon batter into pan. Let rise until double, about 1 hour.

Heat oven to 350°. Bake until golden brown, 50 minutes. Immediately remove from pan.

*Do not use self-rising flour in this recipe.

Like the gardener's green thumb, the white thumb was used to symbolize confidence in baking for this advertising campaign of the early 1960s.

BUCHE de NOEL

3 eggs
1 cup sugar
⅓ cup water
1 teaspoon vanilla
¾ cup Gold Medal all-purpose flour*
1 teaspoon baking powder
¼ teaspoon salt
1 cup chilled whipping cream
2 tablespoons sugar
1½ teaspoons powdered instant coffee
Cocoa Frosting (below)
Red and green candied cherries or chopped pistachio nuts

Heat oven to 375°. Line jelly roll pan, 15½×10½×1 inch, with aluminum foil or waxed paper; grease. Beat eggs in small mixer bowl on high speed until very thick and lemon colored, about 5 minutes. Pour eggs into large mixer bowl; gradually beat in 1 cup sugar. Beat in water and vanilla on low speed. Gradually add flour, baking powder and salt, beating just until batter is smooth. Pour into pan, spreading batter to corners.

Bake until wooden pick inserted in center comes out clean, 12 to 15 minutes. Loosen cake from edges of pan; immediately invert on towel generously sprinkled with powdered sugar. Remove foil; trim stiff edges of cake if necessary. While hot, roll cake and towel from narrow end. Cool on wire rack at least 30 minutes.

Beat whipping cream, 2 tablespoons sugar and the coffee in chilled bowl until stiff. Unroll cake; remove towel. Spread whipped cream mixture over cake. Roll up; frost with Cocoa Frosting. Make strokes with tines of fork to resemble bark. Decorate with holly rope made from cherries or sprinkle with nuts. Store in refrigerator.   10 servings.

*If using self-rising flour, omit baking powder and salt.

Cocoa Frosting

⅓ cup cocoa
⅓ cup margarine or butter, softened
2 cups powdered sugar
1½ teaspoons vanilla
1 to 2 tablespoons hot water

Mix cocoa and margarine. Stir in powdered sugar. Beat in vanilla and water until smooth and of spreading consistency.

A 1940 survey revealed that 9 out of 10 homemakers knew who Betty Crocker was. And once, Betty Crocker was voted one of America's best known women, second only to Eleanor Roosevelt.

Index